THE
Savvy Mom's
GUIDE
TO SONS

101 REAL-WORLD TIPS
TO IMPROVE YOUR RELATIONSHIP—
AND SAVE YOUR SANITY

Tina Krause

SHILOH RUN PRESS

Cover Design: Greg Jackson, Thinkpen Design

Published by Shiloh Run Press, an imprint of Barbour Publishing, Inc., P.O. Box 719, Uhrichsville, Ohio 44683, www.shilohrunpress.com.

Our mission is to publish and distribute inspirational products offering exceptional value and biblical encouragement to the masses.

 Member of the
Evangelical Christian
Publishers Association

Printed in the United States of America.

Contents

Start Here

Why are boys so rambunctious? What draws little boys to mischievous play and daring adventures? Why do boys act and talk the way they do? How do they think and feel? How do I handle my son's teenage years? What about peer pressure? How do I release him into the world?

These are only a few of the questions mothers of sons ponder as they grow their little boys into men. Raising a son takes a lot of savvy, a ton of patience and endurance, a truckload of humor, and a generalized—albeit murky—understanding of what makes a boy tick!

The Savvy Mom's Guide to Sons provides 101 commonsense, real-world tips to mothers of boys. From the cradle to the college dorm, from his first step to the day he walks his bride down the aisle, this guide is intended to help you along your parenting journey.

Each tip comes with:

♡ A Word from the Word—a relevant and revelatory scripture verse,

♡ Think About It—practical questions and suggestions regarding that tip, and

♡ Final Thoughts—some last words on the subject at hand.

The tips are in chronological order to make it easy for you to reference suggestions applicable to your son's age or stage of development. For example, Tip 1 begins at the beginning—the moment you first hold your son in your arms and imagine who and what he will become. As he delights and beguiles you, you will travel through the terrible twos and those precious toddler moments that will incite giggles one moment and produce havoc the next.

Tip 19 and beyond transitions from the holding stage into the molding stage—those formative elementary school years that lead into adolescence. You will retrieve action figures from the toilet, make mud pies even though you hate the mess, and catch lightning bugs (and various other insects) in a jar. He will charm you and drive you crazy all at the same time.

Enter puberty at Tip 55 when changes in your son's voice, appearance, and attitude shift faster than a race car in full throttle. Your little boy inches toward adulthood, and the transition is sobering as an ice bath. But he's still loveable, bright, and your pride and joy.

Finally, Tip 88 ushers you along the road to letting go of your son as he leaves home for college, a job, or military service. You purchase everything he'll need (and much more) to help him to nest in his new living quarters while your nest feels emptier than a discarded soup can. Everything within you hangs on, longing for the "holding" days until you realize that as God severs the ties, He also soothes the wrinkles—the ones on your face and in your heart—weaving a new pattern to your son's life and to yours.

The *Savvy Mom's Guide to Sons* is designed to help you at whatever stage you are in, to hold, mold, or let go of your son. Whether he is five or fifteen, this book will provide some much-needed insights worth considering. So read on and, as you do, enjoy the journey!

Note: Many of the following tips refer to your husband or your son's dad as a helpful participant in the parenting process. . .though for various reasons, we know that many women are raising sons on their own. If this is your situation, please accept my best wishes. . .and substitute "close friend or relative" as needed.

1. Master the skill of juggling; it'll come in handy.

Perhaps you are a new mom of a bouncing baby boy. If so, you are about to board the train for the most exciting, wonderful, exasperating, rewarding, overwhelming, worrisome, and exhausting journey of your life. In fact, don't be embarrassed or think it abnormal if one day you find that you are the poor woman the store manager refers to when he announces: "Attention shoppers, we have a lost mother in the store. If you should find her, be kind and point her back home."

Tackling the multifaceted roles of motherhood is like juggling twenty hats in the air at once. It is a lifelong journey, or as one wise woman said: "Motherhood is a life sentence with no hope of parole." A mere few months of motherhood establishes an inevitable fact: Like the hick-town mayor of a small community, moms wear a number of different hats in their never-ending and ever-growing role as mom.

Growing into motherhood, you will become quite skilled at hat juggling. To illustrate, consider a few of these headpieces: You serve as a nurse, maid, waitress, chauffeur, chef, preacher, teacher, scholar (with a degree in experience), seamstress, referee, cheerleader, coach, and prayer warrior. In each of these roles, you will exercise the wisdom of Solomon, the patience of Job, the faith of Abraham, and the unconditional love of God.

Mothering sons is hard work splashed with colorful strokes of joy. After finding his parents' wedding album, one little boy innocently turned to his dad and asked, "Daddy, is that the day you got Mom to come and work for us?" That's pretty much how it feels sometimes. Your son will lead you through mountains of laundry, fields of dandelions, dirty diaper paths, rock-n-roll roads, rivers of tears, highways of heartaches, jagged childhood crevices, narrow tunnels of worry, junctions of pride and joy, and oceans—definitely oceans—of prayer.

But as you juggle all of those hats, assume all those roles, and travel the various highways and byways, remember God has equipped you for the job. He has gifted you with the most precious treasure of all: a bouncing (running, jumping, climbing) baby boy. He's entrusted you to hold and mold him into a person of character, integrity, and strength so he will fulfill the individual plan God has for him. Most of all, remember you won't have to go it alone. The Lord will give you the wisdom, strength, and direction you need in your journey.

If you lack any of these juggling skills, be assured you'll learn them along the way. Your son will make sure of that!

A WORD FROM THE WORD:

Then they can urge the younger women to love their husbands and children, to be self-controlled and pure, to be busy at home.
Titus 2:4–5 NIV

Think About It. . .

- ♡ Moms need time-outs, too. Whenever your hat-juggling becomes too much, take time out for yourself, even if it's just an hour.

- ♡ Okay, so a few of your "hats" fell to the ground. Don't fret. No one becomes proficient in any skill without lots of mistakes, fumbles, and mishaps.

- ♡ Hold your new son while you can. Before long, he'll be running headlong in any and all directions.

FINAL THOUGHTS:

Motherhood is a tough job. Your son comes with no instruction manual or explicit directions attached to his tiny toes. You learn as you go along. God's Word is your source of reference, and the Lord is your teacher and advocate as He administers just what you need when you need it most. Often, what you need is just a thirty-minute nap! Regardless, remember that with God, you are *already* equipped to raise this little baby boy into the man God desires.

2. Learn with him and about him.

Are you the mom of a firstborn son? You may feel like a slow starter, but you are a quick study. You have to be. Your baby boy is the cutest little creature in all of God's creation. He coos and babbles, and your heart melts. Swaddled in a receiving blanket you struggled to wrap him in, he sleeps peacefully in your arms. Although his first smile is the result of gas elimination (one of many eliminations to come), you are convinced that he directed his grin toward the adoring face of his mommy.

Soon, you learn that he runs the show. He sets the rules and establishes the timetable. You leap to his crying commands every waking—and sleeping—hour. You feed, burp, change diapers, feed, burp, change diapers, bathe him and wash his clothes, scurry to cook something eatable for your husband, and attempt to squeeze in a five-minute nap.

And so the school of honing motherly experiences begins. Here are a few tips within this tip to sharpen your skill set.

- ♡ Lesson 1 with baby boys: Hold another diaper or cloth over his penis while changing him or you'll end up with pee in the face and/or on your pajamas in the middle of the night. There is nothing like an unexpected spray to the face to wake up a sleepy mom.

- ♡ Lesson 2: Don't expect to sleep until your son leaves home. (Just kidding. . .well, sort of.) Sleep when you can and let the housework go. This is tough for some of us who stress over a bread crumb on the counter. But you'll soon learn that your housecleaning efforts are the least of your concerns. Baby takes precedence.

- ♡ Lesson 3: Enjoy everything about him (after you get some much-needed sleep). This is your bonding time—just you and your son. There will never be another stage like this one. This is the holding phase of his development: the time when he not only allows, but thrives and depends on you to nurture and care for him. Helpless, defenseless, pure, and precious is your baby boy. Hold him while you can.

You are learning as he learns. You view life differently now because it *is* different; you are different. You're the mom of a beautiful baby boy. In the months and years to come, you'll embrace tender, joyful, and heartwarming moments; endure difficult challenges; and create and store a treasure-trove of memories. Much like Jesus' mother Mary, you'll "ponder" all of these things in your heart. So relax. You don't need to know everything now. He will learn and so will you.

A WORD FROM THE WORD:

What you learn from them will crown you with grace and be a chain of honor around your neck
PROVERBS 1:9 NLT

Think About It. . .

♡ Are you drained and overwhelmed? Remember, you're not alone. Ask for help. Your mom, mother-in-law, sister, and friends are available if you need them. Don't be afraid to ask.

♡ Babies make messes, and new moms mess up sometimes. It's part of the learning curve. Don't fret; you're human. Learn and go on.

♡ Establish a schedule for your baby boy. Set a daily routine for feeding, bathing, sleeping, and so on, then stick to it. That way, he'll know what to expect, and you will, too, enabling you to plan ahead.

FINAL THOUGHTS:

If you haven't heard it already, you will very soon: "Enjoy them while they're small," well-meaning moms and grandmas advise. Meanwhile, you nod off with bags under your eyes and spit-up stains on your shoulder. You thank God for your new baby and you want to enjoy him; but right now is not a good time to get slathered with trite, albeit true, directives. So allow yourself room to grow and space to experience new motherhood. You have much to teach your son, and along the way he'll teach you, too.

● ●

3. Nap when he naps.

● ●

Your son keeps you hopping. So much so that it's hard to maintain your normal daily household chores. So the thought of napping when he naps seems absurd, and a giant waste of time. Here's a reality check: It's not a waste of time; it's necessary.

Someone once said, "Being a young mother doesn't mean that my life is over. It simply means my life starts a little earlier." Yes, those middle-of-the-night feedings and early morning starts can drain the stamina of the most energized among us. Training for a marathon is a walk in the park compared to the grueling ultra-marathon runs you accomplish caring for your new son. The constant attention your infant requires zaps your strength in no time.

Sleep deprived, you morph into a walking zombie. Forget makeup, hair, and those beauty regimens that you once did routinely before ever stepping into the light of day. New moms hardly have enough time to change out of their pajamas, let alone apply makeup. Besides, who cares? You're too tired!

Thus, the "nap when he naps" tip. Before you fall apart—like a stack of wooden blocks in the hands of a toddler—snooze whenever you can squeeze it in. If you need help, talk to your husband about his handling a few middle-of-the-night feedings so you can restore your sleep needs. Don't wait until you've reached your limit. Leave the laundry, dirty dishes, and dust, and nap when your baby naps. The chores can wait; he cannot.

Your inner alarm and/or your screaming baby will wake you, so don't worry about dozing off and not hearing him. You will.

To deprive yourself of sleep and ignore your body's warning signs is to position yourself for depression and the "baby blues." Moody moms make for major mayhem. So ask for help; that's what your baby's grandparents are for. If your family lives too far from you, solicit the help of a friend or a trustworthy older lady, perhaps from your church. Any mom, whatever the age, remembers those hectic early years and will gladly offer a hand.

Keep in mind that this crazy schedule of yours won't last forever. Soon, your precious son will sleep through the night. Really, he will. Meanwhile, catch a few z's when you can. If not, you might just be ready for the funny farm by the time he reaches six months old. And there are enough worn-out moms residing there already.

A WORD FROM THE WORD:

It is useless for you to work so hard from early morning until late at night. . .for God gives rest to his loved ones.
PSALM 127:2 NLT

Think About It. . .

- ♡ God is the only one who doesn't require sleep. You do, and often. New moms especially.

- ♡ So you think you'll "rest" for a few minutes and that will take care of your sleep deprivation? Nope. According to the National Sleep Foundation, the average adult requires seven to nine hours of sleep daily. To rest is great; to sleep is better.

- ♡ Before you lie down to nap, shut off your phone, darken the room, and determine that this is your time. Then sleep like a baby—yours!

Ralph Waldo Emerson wrote: "There was never a child so lovely but his mother was glad to get him to sleep." You adore your little son, but you love it when he sleeps. When he's off in la-la land, you can enjoy a much-needed reprieve. So take the time and use it wisely. Sleep is an inborn tranquilizer, restorer, and tension easer. Adequate snoozing makes you a better mom. So for your sake, your family's, and your newborn's—sleep.

• •

4. Mother, don't smother.

• •

We nestle our son in our arms, examining his tiny toes and fingers. We wonder what kind of man he'll become. Soon after, we realize that holding him is more than the joy of swaddling him in our arms. Our instinctive nature to nurture, protect, and care for him has kicked in. Holding means we give unselfishly and openly—we deposit ourselves into his life, placing his needs before our own.

When our sons are young, we have full control. We nurture, feed, clothe, cuddle, and comfort them. Our social calendar consists of middle-of-the-night feedings and unexpected trips to the pediatrician. Soon we exchange breast-feeding with baseball games and unexpected trips to the emergency room. When they hurt, we hurt worse than they do.

Call it a misfiring of the feminine brain, an out-of-control hormonal defect, or an over-exaggerated burst of maternal instincts, but we will protect our son at any and all costs. Even at the risk of slipping into the inapt posture of overprotection. But moms beware: Our overprotective nature can hold our sons hostage in a bubble of mother-smother—that icky mixture of control and fear that overwhelms our common sense.

So when do we cross the line from mothering to smothering? It begins early. Consider this commonplace scenario: Your three-year-old son runs in to a wall, bounces off, falls to the floor, and rises unaffected, determined to go on his way. Meanwhile, you're aghast!

"Sweetie!" you shout breathlessly, running to his side, "Are you okay?" But he's already off and running, leaving you an emotional basket case.

Enter elementary school age: Your son starts to distance himself from you, primarily around his friends. You lather on the affection, but he shuns outward expressions of your love. Don't take it personally; it's part of his development. Save the hugs and kisses for home and allow him to maintain his boyish reputation among his peers.

Then the tween and teenage years: Avoid embarrassing him at all cost! That means withholding statements like: "Be careful. Don't get hurt!" as he joins his soccer team for a game. And forget about announcing, "I love you, honey!" in public. Your son needs (and wants) your love and protection in the right place, at the right time, in the proper manner, and in certain situations.

Smothering suffocates and stifles your son's growth. Don't rescue him out of every mess. The biblical mom helps her son to grow and mature; she coaches him to learn from his mistakes (and lets him make them); she guides him with wisdom and prays for him to reach his full potential in Christ.

House rules, rule. It's our job to play an active role, but not an overly intrusive one as our sons mature. Protect his innocence at all times; monitor the movies or television programs he watches and the video games he plays; screen the books he reads and limit and oversee his computer time. Get to know his friends. Be your son's advocate, not his fairy godmother. Mother, don't smother.

A WORD FROM THE WORD:

He will cover you with his feathers. He will shelter you with his wings. His faithful promises are your armor and protection.
PSALM 91:4 NLT

Think About It. . .

♡ Do you run to your son's rescue anytime he fails or falls? Do you shelter him from pain, even if his pain is self-inflicted? If the answers are yes, surrender your son to God in prayer and seek His wisdom and direction. He'll give it.

- ♡ Avoid excessive hovering. It's as annoying to your son as a swarm of pesky flies are to you.

- ♡ Examine ways you can mother without smothering. Take your toddler to the park and let him run and climb (within limits). Talk to your son without nagging. Listen without overreacting. Teach, don't preach. Allow him to take reasonable risks (even though you're doing so with clenched teeth and held breath).

FINAL THOUGHTS:

Oprah once wisely noted that being a mother is the hardest job in the world. Mothering isn't for wimps! You walk a fine line—a real balancing act. Yet God's promises are true, and as you stand on His Word, you need not worry about your son's protection. God already has him covered.

5. He learns through repetition. So oblige him with encores.

Have you noticed that repeated silly gestures make your twelve-month-old son dissolve into giggles? He never tires of repetition; in fact, he begs for and delights in encores.

We all have little games we play with our toddlers. Take, for instance, the stinky feet game. Hold your son and say, "I smell something" as you make sniffing sounds and reach for his tiny foot. Foot to nose, take an exaggerated whiff and recite, "Stinky feet! Stinky feet!" Watch him dissolve into hearty giggles as he pulls his foot away and buries his head into your shoulder. A few seconds later, he extends his foot, eager for you to repeat the exchange once again.

Little boys love repetition. How many times has your toddler yelled, "Do it again!" as you twirl him in the air, feet flying off the ground? Monotonously, you oblige until you halt in breathless exhaustion. Meanwhile, he craves more of the same.

Lessons are taught through repetition. Sometimes, though, we adults prefer to avoid repetition; its allure depreciates with time and use. Our small sons, on the other hand, thrive on it.

So why not look for meaning in the mundane? This is an area in which your toddler can teach you. He derives pleasure, laughter, and interest in the smallest of things. So enjoy his enjoyments.

After all, how many times has our heavenly Father had to repeat the same message to our hearts? Just as a child goes through different stages of growth, so do we. Repetition deposits lessons into our memory bank. That's why the Bible never becomes redundant. We may read the same scripture or inspirational thought repeatedly, but it seems brand-new when God uses it to speak to us.

Remaining childlike is essential to our spiritual growth, just as your son's childish games are essential to his physical and emotional growth. The only difference? Unlike us, our heavenly Father never tires of our pleas for an encore.

A WORD FROM THE WORD:

At that time Jesus said, "I praise you, Father, Lord of heaven and earth, because you have hidden these things from the wise and learned, and revealed them to little children."
MATTHEW 11:25 NIV

Think About It. . .

♡ Learning is taught and engrained through repetition. How else will your child learn the alphabet or multiplication tables? How did you learn them? That's right, constant repetition.

♡ Repeat a Bible verse daily to memorize scripture. Use index cards as cheat sheets. Unlike the stinky feet game, this kind of repetition need not exhaust you.

♡ Through your repetitive actions and words, your child takes note. If you routinely read your Bible, he will, too. If you use proper manners, he'll catch on. Keep on keeping on, Mom. Your son will benefit from your routine of positive example.

FINAL THOUGHTS:

One day your son will be too old for the repetition of childish games. He might even call them "lame." But God never tires of your repeated requests and pleas. In fact, He waits for you to turn to Him. Just like your small son, you learn from repeated experience.

• •

6. Whenever possible, avoid eating on the run as you run after your active son.

• •

"You should weigh ninety-eight pounds the way you run around," a dad told his adult daughter during a visit to her home.

Deb was the mom of a two-year-old son—a little guy who behaved as if a perpetual sugar surge propelled him. She was in constant motion in sync with her active son. "Yeah, you'd think I'd lose weight instead of piling on the pounds," she responded, scooping her son into her arms.

It's bad enough to gain unwanted pregnancy pounds, but that's rarely the end of it. Many moms fall into the eat-on-the-run pattern early on. It begins when your son is born and continues until the day you catch a glimpse of your widening waist in the reflection of a store window. Or, jeans that once zipped up with ease hardly pass your hips without shimmying the denim back and forth with a hearty pull. Then reality hits. The pounds are a result of mindless eating. The aha moment shocks and appalls you at the same time. *How did I get this way? What happened to me?*

The answer is simple: motherhood. New moms maintain crazy lifestyles. You're up most of the night, nap when you can during the day, and make an all-out attempt to juggle and maintain the rest of your responsibilities. Eating becomes mindless. For instance: Your son finally naps, so you rush to complete unfinished tasks that are impossible to accomplish while he is awake. Finally, you sit down to eat. Right on cue, he's awake and your attention focuses on him instead. He's hungry, so you prepare him lunch as you take bites of your sandwich in between. He doesn't eat everything, so you finish his leftovers as you scrape the dishes and clear the table.

This type of eat-on-the-go snacking goes on all day. Your toddler gets Goldfish crackers and so do you; you make dinner and nibble along the way, and before long you've consumed enough calories to cause an ant to bulge beetle-size, yet it seems as if you've eaten nothing at all. Sit-down meals become obsolete, because even when you do sit down, you jump up and down from the table to wipe your toddler's face or pour him more juice. Or just when you think you have time to relax and enjoy a meal, your toddler fusses and you're on the run again. Sound familiar?

Moms need some quiet time to eat a meal slowly; instead, we gobble food into our mouths faster than a fat man at a pie-eating contest. Over time, we are habitual fast eaters. Throw in some convenience food, and we evolve into fast-food eaters eating fast. "One chicken nugget Happy Meal and a double cheeseburger with fries, please," we recite at the drive-through window. Then we end up ingesting the chicken nuggets our son didn't eat, as well as our own cheeseburger and fries.

For some of us, the hectic, nonstop pace of motherhood becomes the bane of our weight-watching existence. Nervous eating replaces normal eating practices. It all comes with new motherhood like chicken nuggets come with your choice of sauce.

If this is your current dilemma, don't lose hope. Try these suggestions: Take time to assess your eating habits. When do you eat the most? Do you snack when your son does? Are you prone to eat on the run or finish your child's food? Then make a plan. Schedule your mealtimes (I realize this means more work, but stay with me). Feed your son first, then eat after he's settled into watching a video or occupied with confined playing so you don't have to worry he'll get into something. Or plan your meals while he sleeps. Eat first, then do chores or take a nap. (See Tip 3.) Slow down. Deliberately chew your food, instead of gulping and swallowing big bites. Don't eat convenience food, no matter how tempting.

Nervous, mindless eating is a common problem, but it is solvable with a little concentrated effort. When all else fails, remember that your baby won't be a toddler for long. Meanwhile watch, don't eat, those Goldfish crackers.

A WORD FROM THE WORD:

The wise store up choice food and olive oil,
but fools gulp theirs down.
PROVERBS 21:20 NIV

Think About It. . .

♡ Is your self-control uncontrolled? Do you have poor eating habits? For one day, record everything you put in your mouth. People often deceive themselves into thinking they eat a lot less than they really do.

♡ With all of the things you have to do each day, eating is one of your only pleasures. But in the long run it makes you unhappy as you beat yourself up for overeating. The extra pounds are a constant reminder of out-of-control eating. Find pleasures in the positives. Take some time for yourself. Regroup. Relax. Reschedule. Find a temporary respite to breathe and gain perspective.

FINAL THOUGHTS:

Remember the familiar saying, "A man may work from sun to sun, but a woman's work is never done"? Chasing your active son is exhausting. He has so many needs for you to fulfill while you shoulder other pending chores, errands, and activities. No wonder some moms turn to food as a pacifier amid the chaoitc pace of motherhood. Believe it or not, God understands. He's there to help you with whatever, wherever you need Him. The Bible says He even puts a guard on your mouth! (See Psalm 141:3.)

7. Record your son's stages of development and milestones.

As a new mom, you're busy. *Real* busy! Nevertheless, you'll thank yourself later if you remember to record your son's milestones today. Take lots of photos, and video special occasions and cute encounters. Most of us are diligent about that with our firstborn, but our picture/ video taking wanes more with the birth of each child after that.

Keep keepsakes such as your son's first piece of artwork, awards, and preschool papers of significance (I have a suitcase filled with them). I still treasure the story my son wrote about the day his brother fell into our tomato patch, and the prose my other son penned about what he loved most about his mom. *Sigh.* After my first grandson, Ian, was born, I kept a computer file named "Ian's Updates," where I recorded some of the cutest things he said and did—things I'd surely forget by now. And I kept and cherish both my son's and his son's kindergarten graduation caps. My son and grandson both attended the same Christian school and even had the same kindergarten teacher! Although the homemade caps were made of basic white poster board with golden yarn tassels, they are priceless to me.

When Ian was three or four years old, he found a rusty washer on the street as we walked the neighborhood. To him, it was gold. Nearby was a large fountain, and I held his hand as he walked atop the base of it, clutching his special find in his tiny fist. Without warning, plop! The washer fell into the murky water. He was devastated. Choking back the tears, he leaned against a tree. With eyes closed and hands clasped, he prayed in a whisper asking God to help his Nana—who probably looked, and felt, as if she lost her diamond ring—find his newfound treasure that now rested at the bottom of the concrete fountain.

I sat on the ledge and looked to see if I could locate it on the bottom. *Oh Lord,* I thought in a panic, *You have to help me find that washer.* As my grandson prayed, I was determined to answer his prayer. So much for unfeigned faith! So with eyes wide open I held my breath, bent over, and submerged my entire head into three feet of dirty water, visually surveying the bottom for Ian's lost treasure. Nothing. Coming up for air, I gazed at Ian still standing by the tree, praying. So I plunged in again and God mercifully answered both of our prayers.

Hair dripping dirty water into my face, I handed the rusty washer to my grandson and told him how we needed to thank Jesus for answering his prayer. Ian is seventeen years old now and beneath piles of boxed scribbled artwork and clay projects rests that treasured rusty washer.

You, too, will endear yourself to what your son holds closely: The stuffed animal your toddler sleeps with or his favorite toy or storybook.

Start a baby book when your child is born, and record his height and weight at different ages. Journal special moments like his first word and his favorite foods. Record the day he lost his first tooth or took his first step. Include the day you dedicated him to the Lord. Construct a chart on the back of a door to record his growth. Save meaningful, heartfelt items and bundle them into tangible reminders of your son's childhood.

A WORD FROM THE WORD:

Let this be recorded for future generations,
so that a people not yet born will praise the Lord.
PSALM 102:18 NLT

Think About It. . .

💗 Baby books are invaluable resources in which to read and retrieve precious memories. Nice ones include places for baby's hospital bracelet and lock of hair from his first haircut. You can find these books in Hallmark stores or on the Internet.

💗 Can you think of ways to journal your thoughts about your son? Start today. Years from now you'll be glad you did.

♡ Remember to date everything from photos to artwork. Your memory may fail you years from now.

FINAL THOUGHTS:

Imagine if God's prophets and apostles had failed to record the works of the Lord. Scripture encourages believers to record special events and the faithful fulfillment of God's promises to them. How would anyone know the genealogy of Christ and His ancestors if it weren't for the handwritten records of God's people?

Your son is one of the most precious gifts God will ever give you. Today's technology affords you easy and convenient ways to record your memories. Capture every moment on paper, computer files, video tape, cell phones, and good old-fashioned photographs.

• •

8. Securely strap him in—when he's not looking.

• •

Boys are ingenious when it serves their purpose. Your innovative creation begins early to learn the ins and outs of making his way through, over, under, and behind objects of interest. They also have a knack for discovering simple ways to escape any tight spots.

The jail inmate who masterminded the 1962 great escape from Alcatraz—the most highly monitored and secured prison—has little over your little one. He can and does maneuver himself loose from car seats with five-point systems. Even harnesses that hug our bodies tauter than a body builder's abs and strollers built to keep kids' bottoms in a seated position at all times can't contain him.

Have you ever let your toddler loose from his stroller and then battled to get him back in it? With stiffened torso, legs kicking and arms flaying, he shrieks in horror as if you've just entered the doctor's office for a round of vaccinations.

It didn't take one toddler long to learn—after watching his mom intently—that *click* meant strapped in and can't move anywhere;

meanwhile the red button meant one hardy push and he can stand up, climb, better yet, take over the vehicle. It took a few attempts to push just hard enough and then voilá—he was loose! All sense of security vanished while his mom scrambled to restrain him.

Ah yes, the lesson here is to distract your toddler while anchoring him securely. Because should he notice what you're doing (and he will eventually), you're in for years of pulling your automobile to an abrupt and dangerous halt to jump out, careen into the backseat, and reattach him to safety.

The same holds true for safety gates, stove and cabinet protectors, and strollers. Avert his eyes while you detach and open or you'll soon wake up to find him bouncing down the stairs to the kitchen to play with some pots, pans, and stove handles while you're fast asleep. And we won't even attempt to describe the dangerous dealings of a small child loosening shopping cart straps and then standing on top of the seat mere seconds after his mom turns to reach for a jar of peanut butter.

One of the most important jobs we have as a mom is maintaining a safe environment for our children in and outside of the home. Protecting your son from his own devices is a daunting but doable task. There is so much for him to discover, but it is up to you to limit and monitor his many explorations.

Safety is first and foremost with your young son. Don't put anything past him. Secure bookshelves and television sets; childproof your home with plastic inserts for electrical outlets; place monitors in his room in case your baby boy tries to scale the prison bars of his crib (mine did at nine months old).

Meanwhile, remain calm. All of these precautionary measures are for the moment. One day you won't have so much childproofing to do. No, your little boy will jump, crawl, or hurl into more interesting adventures.

A WORD FROM THE WORD:

He led me to a place of safety; he rescued
me because he delights in me.
PSALM 18:19 NLT

Think About It...

♡ You delight in and love your son and that's why you protect and rescue him from himself, just as the Lord rescues you. Do you realize you are God's treasured little one? He delights in you daily; He is your place of safety. So relax in His constant care.

♡ How do you divert a child's attention? Before you strap him into safety, point to a tree, a bird, an airplane in the sky. Watch him as he watches you, and be prepared to use some of your own deflective tactics.

♡ Your son understands more than you think. Without initiating unfounded fears, begin early to talk to your son about why he shouldn't unlatch his seat belt or open cabinet drawers. Establish your authority.

♡ Is your son overactive? Give him activity books, small toys, or play a sing-along CD to keep him occupied in the car. Play road games like I Spy or ask: "Can you find things that are the color blue?"

FINAL THOUGHTS:

In this increasingly unstable and unsafe environment called Earth, your challenge to keep your son safe is a daily quest. Yet the scriptures say that after you've done everything you know to do, you are to stand firmly on God's promises. You can't avoid every accident; you can only do your best to avoid it. Learn to pray for and with your son often to avert potential disasters.

9. Expect the unexpected from your toddler. Then hand him to his daddy.

She needed a birthday gift for a friend and decided to take her two-year-old son, Billy—the poster child for the terrible twos—to the store. Suffice it to say it was the last time she would do so, until he reached the ripe old age of three. Here's what happened.

To avoid dragging along a stroller, this innocent mom led her toddler by the hand and entered the store. Ditching the stroller was her first mistake. Instead of struggling with the baby carriage, she struggled with her son. Billy plopped down on his bottom and, like a stubborn mule, refused to budge. Frustrated, his mom lifted him with both hands as he whined, squirmed, and kicked until she put him down. The moment his feet hit the linoleum, he hunkered down again. It was as if his bottom was cemented to the floor. Meanwhile, she issued stern directives, "Billy, stop it! Stand up! Do you want a time-out?"

He finally rose to his feet and she tugged him along to the rack of blouses. Immediately he darted beneath them. His mom, now on all fours, raced after him, catching him just before his tiny body was lost in a sea of clothing. Lifting him to straddle her hip lasted seconds before he squirmed his way down her leg and back in motion. For a moment, she ignored him to gather a few seconds to actually look at a blouse. That's when it happened.

"My display!" the saleslady yelled, racing to the storefront window. There was darling little Billy flinging items, just before he pushed over a mannequin. His mom darted toward him as the woman said sternly, "I'll get him!" I'll get him as in haven't-you-and-your-little-brat–done-enough-damage, I'll get him. Fortunately, Mom managed to retrieve him before the saleslady did. Onlookers gawked as the miniature bulldozer and his red-faced mom slid toward the exit faster than a racing bobsled.

Exhausted, frustrated, angry, and just plain fed-up, she arrived at home, confronted her husband, and with outstretched arms handed her son to him saying, "Here, *you* take him! I've had enough!" The bewildered dad held his son as mom slammed the bedroom door to rest and regroup.

Expect the unexpected with your toddlers. They are investigators and instigators by nature. Little Billy never meant to throw his mommy into a complete meltdown. He was just being a normal boy, interested in much more than shopping for blouses and other nonsense. Why not toss a few items in the air? Or knock down a fiberglass lady and see if she gets up?

Little boys will test our wills and patience. After a heavy dose of it, we need to know when to turn them over to Dada, Nana, Papa, or anyone who can give us a reprieve and help us gather our wits after our little bulldozer outwits us.

A WORD FROM THE WORD:

What more could I have done for my vineyard that I have not already done? When I expected sweet grapes, why did my vineyard give me bitter grapes?
ISAIAH 5:4 NLT

Think About It. . .

♡ Some days you'll feel as if your little sweetie turned sour on you, just like the grapes in Isaiah 5. Toddlers are discovering the world around them. To them, everything is a reason to explore. Expect your boy to grab and squirm out of your arms when something interesting catches his eye or when he simply gets the urge to break loose into freedom. That's normal, although dismantling a storefront window is not.

♡ Prepare for delays at the airport, long lines, heavy traffic, and all the things that can happen with your toddler during waiting periods. Take sufficient toys and snacks to occupy him. Use the stroller as much as possible. So when the unexpected happens—and it will—hopefully, you'll be prepared.

♡ What unexpected act has your toddler surprised you with

in the past? What did it teach you? How did you handle it? How did it prepare you to handle similar situations in the future?

Zig Ziglar reminds us, "Expect the best; prepare for the worst." Not bad advice for moms with sons on the run. Your son is your joy. He brings you far more happiness than he does displeasure. But when he does act up in the most humiliating of ways, it's time to regroup and assess the situation for future reference. Thank God for dads who are ready to take over before we lurch into physical and emotional combustion.

• •

10. Remember, it may feel like a job, but motherhood is a ministry.

• •

One mom nailed it when she said, "If motherhood was meant to be easy, it never would have started with something called labor." Yep, that should have been our first clue. Raising a son isn't easy.

Karen, a mother of two boys, remembered one day in particular when motherhood had taken its toll. The mere thought of one more sibling argument, one more spilled juice drink, one more demand on her time, or one more whining voice answering back, "But I don't want to!" would have sent her over the edge.

Her two small boys had managed to assault her central nervous system with a barrage of chaos and confusion. She was about to explode when the words of Jesus intrusively invaded her thoughts. "Let the little children to come to Me, and do not forbid them" (Luke 18:16 NKJV).

Not exactly what I want to hear, she moaned within. But she knew it was time to pray. So she went to the bathroom (Note: Whoever named that tiled sanctuary a "restroom" must have been a mom. It's the only place in the house to get rest away from the kids—at least for a few minutes). Sitting on the edge of the bathtub, Karen prayed, "Lord, do you realize how tough being a mom is? I do everything around here, and what thanks do I get?"

Within minutes, God silenced her thoughts with pictures of the past: The time she laid sick in bed, praying for healing. Surprisingly, the next day she'd felt rested and refreshed. "Must have been the Tylenol I took," she'd surmised. Then she thought about the time she had felt pressured, panicked, and alone, pleading, "Please, Lord. Tell me what to do." And how afterward a peace had settled her anxieties and God had given her clear direction. Yet instead of praising Him, she had attributed it to her own ingenuity and wisdom.

In that moment, sitting on the edge of the tub, Karen realized that God *does* understand moms. He cleans up their messes, bandages their wounds, delivers them to destinations safely, heals their sick bodies, and comforts their broken hearts. And often, *He* never receives a thank you.

Motherhood is a ministry. It involves endless acts of sacrificial love, which are often received with little or no appreciation. But we have the reward of knowing that we are doing our best to mold, direct, teach, comfort, heal, and touch our sons' lives so they, in turn, will someday do the same for others.

Author Sandra Aldrich said, "Our little ones won't be with us forever. When they're grown, they won't remember whether they had size one designer jeans or a solid-maple crib. But they will remember, even subconsciously, whether they were loved and protected."

So labor on, Mom. Your work is not in vain. After all, God knows a little bit about labor, too. Just look how much He has toiled over you. By the way, have you thanked Him today?

A WORD FROM THE WORD:

Therefore, since through God's mercy
we have this ministry, we do not lose heart.
2 CORINTHIANS 4:1 NIV

Think About It. . .

- ♡ Raising hair-raising boys is no easy task. A mom's patience and endurance is tested daily. Do you find yourself overwhelmed by motherhood? If so, be sure to take time apart to pray and do something for yourself. Even Jesus departed from the crowds to get alone with the Father. When you, like Karen, get that one-on-one time with God, He will speak the words you need to hear.

- ♡ Moms spend inordinate amounts of time "doing." Sometimes they need to just "be." Be your son's mom. Slow down; the chores can wait.

- ♡ Motherhood is the hardest and most important role to which women are called. It is their ministry. Ask the Lord for wisdom daily, and depend on Him to supply whatever you need. He never calls you to a task without equipping you to perform it.

FINAL THOUGHTS:

Just as you sacrifice, work, and labor for your son, so does God. How wonderful that He accepts both sons and their mothers as they are—on good days and bad! God views all people as His children. What's more, His arms are always open to those who come to Him with a trusting and childlike faith—for of such is the kingdom of heaven.

• •

11. Establish rules, discipline, and boundaries early.

• •

In anger, your toddler hauls off and smacks you. What do you do?

In the middle of the grocery aisle, he throws himself on the floor kicking and screaming in response to your telling him, "No, you can't have that toy." Now you have an audience of unwelcomed onlookers, and your little boy is the star of the show. How do you draw the curtain?

Your son will test his limits. Children are experts at timing a meltdown in public. These smart little rascals instinctively know where or when you have less control.

There he is, quietly entertaining himself at home for an hour or more, so you decide to pick up the phone. Before you know it, *wham*! He's on you like gum to pavement.

In your son's early years, it seems as if he has *full* control, while your life is one big scrambled egg. For your toddler, anything goes, and he gets into and goes after everything. Now is the time to begin to set age-appropriate boundaries and establish rules. (See Tip 56.)

For instance, grabbing your grandmother's china cups is out of bounds. So is "warming up" to the stove. In a firm, calm manner, establish his boundaries with a "no-no" and immediate removal of, or from, the object of fascination. Teach him that whining does *not* produce immediate gratification, even if you're tempted to buy him the candy bar he's grabbed just to appease him and save yourself embarrassment in the checkout lane.

Establishing rules for your son is necessary for his safety. When my sons were young, we lived in a subdivision with no sidewalks. So the rule was they could play either in the yard or on the driveway with their big wheels or bicycles. Knowing that if they careened into the street their safety was jeopardized, I held to that rule firmly. And they knew early on that disobedience resulted in consequences.

My neighbor also had two boys about the same age, and I'd hear her yelling at her kids regularly to "stay out of the street!" They'd return to the yard only to wander back minutes later. What puzzled me was her lack of consistency. One minute she yelled at them, and the next minute she'd stand by the door while they played in the street, yet she said nothing.

Her sons received mixed messages, namely, "I know Mom doesn't want me to play in the street, but if I do it enough I'll get away with it." And they did.

Consistency in discipline is paramount. If you tell him "no" one minute and allow him to get away with it the next, that communicates that obedience and rules are meaningless. Parents who find it too difficult to establish and stick to rules do their son a huge disservice.

He needs loving, consistent discipline. And if you don't establish it now, it will only get harder later on.

Dr. James Dobson said, "Loving discipline encourages a child to respect other people and live as a responsible, constructive citizen." Okay, so your small boy isn't exactly ready to run for public office or discover a cure for cancer, but one day he might. The loving discipline he receives now will mold him into the godly, productive young man he'll soon become.

God disciplines His children, even baby Christians. He does it from a heart of love and, if we love our little boys, we'll do the same.

A WORD FROM THE WORD:

To discipline a child produces wisdom, but a mother is disgraced by an undisciplined child.
PROVERBS 29:15 NLT

Think About It. . .

♡ Decide what form of discipline is necessary and age-appropriate. Discuss disciplinary actions with your son's father to decide appropriate consequences when your boy disobeys.

♡ Disciplining your child hurts you more than him. It's hard to do, but necessary. Time-outs are great, but if that doesn't work, implement other effective disciplinary measures.

♡ Be consistent. It's often hard to do, especially when you're busy with something else. But your consistency will pay off when you see your son obeying a lot sooner and more often than he did before.

♡ Don't laugh at your young son when he misbehaves. Some of his bad behavior is really cute when he's a toddler but offensive at five years old!

Discipline hurts, and administering it is time consuming. Yet the Word of God instructs parents to discipline their children, just as God disciplines His. If you love your son, you won't allow him to rule the roost and run the household with his bad behavior. Children need structure and the sense of security that loving discipline establishes.

• •

12. Church begins at home. Talk to your son about Jesus.

• •

The Bible instructs us to gather together with other believers to edify, encourage, and support our faith. With that in mind, let's take a mental quiz. Answer true or false: If I'm faithful to take my son to Sunday school, then I've fulfilled my spiritual obligation to bring him up in the fear and admonition of the Lord. If you answered "True," *buzzt.* Wrong.

Instructing and teaching our son begins at birth, and praying for him begins before that. Introducing your young son to Bible stories and Christian-based books helps him understand who God is and how much He loves him. Christian videos and computer applications for children integrate spiritual lessons that toddlers can embrace and understand.

Four-year-old Eric loved to imitate Bible characters, having memorized entire Bible cartoon videos. So when his family vacationed with him in Arizona, he was in his element. The desert landscape provided him with all the props necessary to act out his Bible stories. Gingerly, he neared what looked like a burning bush, minus the flames. With the drama of Charlton Heston, he picked up a stick, approached the bush, threw his makeshift staff to the ground, and pretended to remove his sandals. After all, he was on "holy ground." A tad embarrassed yet blessed at the same time, his mom waited as her little prophet boy acted out the scene.

"He's playing Moses," she offered to onlookers as they strolled past smiling. Later, the little guy used the outdoor cave at the Sonora

Desert Museum as a backdrop for acting out scenes from "Jonah and the Whale."

Eric recited Bible stories like most preschoolers memorize nursery rhymes. Before holiday dinners, he recited the entire Christmas story and listed all the names of Joseph's brothers in the Old Testament. Pretty impressive, huh? All because his parents and grandparents talked about and prayed to the Lord regularly in his presence, and provided him with positive, Christian input and entertainment.

Your son is born with a simple faith and heartfelt innocence, eager to learn about the Lord. Don't make the mistake of waiting for others to teach him about Jesus. What he learns at home from you is far more powerful and lasting than what he'll receive in the classroom or church service.

The nineteenth-century Baptist preacher Charles H. Spurgeon said: "Let no Christian parents fall into the delusion that Sunday school is intended to ease them of their personal duties. The first and most natural condition of things is for Christian parents to train up their own children in the nurture and admonition of the Lord."

Church attendance is important and an integral element to your son's spiritual growth, but faith begins and is nurtured at home.

A WORD FROM THE WORD:

"And you must commit yourselves wholeheartedly to these commands that I am giving you today. Repeat them again and again to your children. Talk about them when you are at home and when you are on the road, when you are going to bed and when you are getting up."
DEUTERONOMY 6:6–7 NLT

Think About It. . .

♡ What do you talk about most? People? Fashions and home décor? Church activities? In the above verse, God commanded parents to talk to their children about Him and the Bible. Whether you are driving down the street in the car or relaxing on the sofa (a rarity, for any mom), talk to your son about Jesus.

♡ Whatever you value most is what you will emulate to your young son. Establish a routine of Bible reading, bedtime prayers, grace before meals, and talking to God about everything. Your son will follow your lead.

FINAL THOUGHTS:

Chances are, your son will act as if he isn't hearing a word you say when you talk about spiritual or scriptural matters. Don't be fooled. He hears you. Before long, seemingly out of nowhere, he will ask something like, "Mommy, why can't we see God?" This is your chance to teach him scriptural truths. Answer him simply, void of unnecessary details he can't handle. Church attendance is important, but nothing takes the place of your daily spiritual nurturing, interaction, and input.

• •

13. If you want to maintain friends and family, keep your son in tow during visits.

• •

Your sister and her husband invite you and your family for a visit. They have no children and you have two, one of whom is a rambunctious, inquisitive little boy. You walk in your sister's door, and your son whizzes around like a miniature tornado, leveling everything in his path. You dash to grab him and he's already located the "untouchables"—a collection of your grandmother's porcelain knickknacks. Snatching a piece of bric-a-brac out of his tiny hand and breathing a sigh of relief, you notice your sister becoming increasingly nervous. And rightly so.

One couple invited its relatives, who had three children under the age of four, to a cookout. When it began to rain, the couple moved the party indoors, and that's when havoc ensued. The three kids ran amok while their parents chatted, seemingly oblivious to the fact that their little ones were on a search and destroy mission and doing it quite successfully. Scraps of food littered the floor, the kids used the couch as a trampoline, and they climbed atop the coffee table. In a few short hours, the hosts' home was destroyed. The nail-biting couple couldn't wait for the guests to leave. And after they did, the exhausted twosome spent hours cleaning up the mess.

Don't abdicate your parental responsibilities when you visit someone's house—relative or not. To do so shows a lack of regard or respect for your hosts. No one knows your child better than you do. So prepare for any visits away from home. Take toys or videos for him to watch to occupy him during the visit. Keep an eye on your little one. If he's a bit older, set down the ground rules beforehand. Even younger children understand unacceptable behavior. And if your son or children are too restless, call it an early night and leave before you overstay your welcome (which just might happen the moment you walk through the door if your son runs rampant).

Be courteous, respectful, and thoughtful. Teach your son that "we don't touch other people's things," and "we eat at the table or kitchen counter, not while running through the house." If you do, you might just get another invitation from your grateful hosts. If not, don't expect the phone to ring anytime soon.

A WORD FROM THE WORD:

Whoever spares the rod hates their children, but the one who loves their children is careful to discipline them.
PROVERBS 13:24 NIV

Think About It...

♡ If relatives invite you to their home, question to see if other children are coming. If not, and you think your son might be overly active or cranky, make plans to leave him at home with a sitter.

♡ Boys will get away with whatever they can. Avoid getting so immersed in conversation that you lose track of what your child is doing. Make sure he has ample items to keep him occupied at someone's home.

Visiting relatives need not turn into a fiasco, so simply avoid allowing a free-for-all. Boys need to learn respect for the possessions and property of others. Teach your son while he's young, and he will exhibit respectful, courteous behavior into adolescence.

• •

14. Enjoy him while he's young, even though you're unsure of what that means!

• •

You've heard it what seems like a million times. The advice usually comes from well-meaning grandmothers or mothers of older children. "Enjoy him while he's young," she says with a gentle smile.

Rewind moments before. You've stopped for a few groceries before driving to pick up your daughter from dance class. Afterward, you have just enough time to get home, put away the groceries, feed your kids a fast dinner, and get ready for midweek church service. You've got a plan and time is ticking away.

Yet your three-year-old son has other ideas. He balks, squirms, whines, and kicks as you place him in the shopping cart. Handing him a toy, you hope to pacify him long enough to get the items on your list. Only in your dreams. He tosses the toy to the floor and reaches for everything along the way as you systematically grab the items out of his hand to place back on the store shelf.

Then it happens. He swipes the boxes of cereal on an endcap and the display tumbles to the floor. Your face flushes with embarrassment and anger all at the same time as you try to reconstruct the tower of cardboard boxes. Meanwhile, your son views this as an opportunity for a great escape. He squirms out of the safety belt and stands to his feet as the cart begins to move with him lunging forward. In the eyes of others you've just morphed into a bad mother of an uncontrollable brat.

You're now fifteen minutes late for picking up your daughter and have visions of her standing teary-eyed, waiting for her absent mom. Seething and anxiety ridden, you make it through checkout when your little tyrant smiles at a sweet elderly lady.

"Oh, he's so cute," she comments.

"Thanks," you blurt out in frustration, thinking, *Oh, lady, if you only knew.* And then it comes.

"They're little for such a short time," she says. "Enjoy him while he's young."

Enjoy him? At that point, what you'd really like to do is string him from his cute little toes!

What does that well-meaning phrase—*enjoy him*—mean anyway? How do you enjoy your little one as he flips a spoonful of mashed potatoes to the floor or deliberately drips grape juice from his sippy cup onto your new carpet? Moms don't enjoy a little boy who throws tantrums, is determined to scale the entertainment center when they're not looking, or hurls toys in fastball fashion.

One quote reads, "Mothers of little boys work from son up to son down." Tangled in the throes and woes of that work, we find it hard to embrace and often recognize the fun stuff. But we really *can* find joy in our journey along the way.

Enjoying your son while he is young is savoring the tender, happy, cute moments he presents. It's thinking about his adorable characteristics and holding him close to your heart. It's embracing his bear hugs and kisses, which will fade with time like fabric in the summer sun. It is cherishing his firsts: First haircut, first word, first step, and first day of school. It's remaining cognizant that he is small for a short period of time before he grows into a full-fledged man.

Philosopher and poet Joan Baez reminded us of how fleeting our son's childhood is when she wrote: "Seeing you sleeping peacefully on your back among your stuffed ducks, bears and basset hounds, would remind me that no matter how good the next day might be, certain moments were gone forever because we could not go backwards in time."

So enjoy him, Mom. Soon you'll wish you could return him to the age he is right now. Really. What's more, one day you'll laugh at his former antics—even the time he razed a tower of cereal boxes at the end of the grocery store aisle.

Think About It. . .

💟 After your son goes to bed, take a mental assessment. Think about all the good things he brings into your life: joy, fun, happiness, adventure. His smile, words, and hugs melt your heart. Ponder those things often.

💟 Take a day and do something special with your toddler. Finger paint a giant poster board. Take him to a community center or YMCA that offers activities for small children and their moms. Enjoy him.

💟 Do you feel so overwhelmed with daily chores, work, and responsibilities that you find it difficult to enjoy the moment? Take time for yourself first and you'll enjoy your toddler more. Did you ever listen to a flight attendant's instructions? In case of an emergency, put on your face mask, then your child's. That goes against our maternal instincts; yet, it makes sense. If you pass out, your child will perish. So take care of yourself for your son's sake.

💟 Think about your son's best characteristics and cutest moments. One day all of that will pass, never to return. Delight in his childlike ways and mannerisms.

FINAL THOUGHTS:

Mary, the mother of Jesus, took a mental note of the various incidents in Jesus' life. She knew He was the Savior, but He was primarily her little Son. She must have had questions—lots of them. But she took one step at a time, raising her Son in a godly household. She pondered what would happen as He grew, who He really was, and what He was sent to do. She thought about Him often and kept her thoughts close to her heart. Like Mary, modern moms ponder similar questions but can also embrace the moment at hand. Cherish the moment: That's the essence of enjoying a son while he's young.

• •

15. If potty training seems impossible, give him a target.

• •

Potty training is overrated. Although it is the bane of every mom's existence (well, one of them, anyway), remember that no one has had to send her son off to college or his first real job in diapers. He *will* get trained. The goal, however, is to potty train your son at a reasonable age of, say, three years old?

Back in the day of cloth diapers—when moms dipped their child's poopy, pee-peed diapers in the toilet by hand, wrung them out, then placed them in a "diaper hamper"—toddlers were typically trained both daytime and at nighttime by age two. Amazing!

Not anymore. Disposable diaper manufacturers have a multibillion-dollar business. (Currently, they've created pull-up diapers up to size five.) They don't want you in a hurry to potty train your child because when your toddler does *his* business where he should, they lose *your* business. But that's a different book.

One mom used a noteworthy idea for potty training her son. "Give him a floating target." Whenever she saw her son squirming and jittering, she'd run to place a flushable object in the toilet. Then she'd position her son, pants down, in front of the commode and tell him to aim for the target. No small boy can resist that! Her son loved it, and he was soon potty trained. But only with pee-pee. Pooping was a target of another bull's-eye.

Her four-year-old son refused to poop in the potty. Instead, when the urge struck, he'd suddenly disappear. After all, adequate privacy is needed. She'd find him in the corner behind the couch, face to corner, doing his duty in his pull-ups.

One time he stayed with his grandparents for the weekend. They decided to take him out of town, and on the way back home he announced he had to poopy. Strapped in a car seat was an unacceptable stance for him since he had become accustomed to standing up during elimination. So his grandparents pulled to the side of the road to accommodate him. They unbuckled him and waited quietly as he stood in the back seat, looking out the window, doing his thing.

His grandma made the mistake of looking over her shoulder to see if he had finished.

"Nana," he stated firmly, "don't look."

"Of course," she giggled. Turning to her husband, she said, "He needs his privacy."

But weeks later, after his mom began making him stay in his dirty pull-ups for a while after pooping, he was soon completely and fully potty trained.

The point of this tip isn't to instruct you how to potty train your son. Everyone has advice, but the truth is what works for one child doesn't necessary hold water (so to speak) with another. Pee puddles and poopy messes are part of the package. But they don't last forever. Eventually, your son will learn to pee in the toilet instead of spraying down the heat registers or watering the flowers in the garden.

Of course, for the next fifteen years after that, prepare to sit on wet toilet seats. And expect an occasional, impromptu, middle-of-the night plunge into the toilet after one of your boys forgets to lower the toilet seat after using it. Another heads-up: Prepare for frequent cleanups of urine on, in, behind, next to, and under the toilet. After your son learns no visible target exists, he'll get pretty sloppy about aiming in the right direction.

But don't fret. That, too, will pass, even though right now it seems like your son won't ever hit the target. What seems like a monsoon to us is but a sprinkle in the grand scheme of things.

A WORD FROM THE WORD:

But do not forget this one thing, dear friends: With the Lord a day is like a thousand years, and a thousand years are like a day.

2 PETER 3:8 NIV

Think About It . . .

- ♡ Potty training your son is frustrating and creates anxiety, especially after you have tried everything and seemingly failed. Just be sure not to push your toddler or a battle of the wills is sure to ensue.

- ♡ Collect sound advice but let your gut lead you. Every child is different. Try different techniques, and when you find one that works, stick with it.

- ♡ Be consistent.

FINAL THOUGHTS:

More moms have anguished over potty training than anything else. Well, at least until their son reaches puberty. The key is to exercise patience and consistency. In other words, stay on top of the matter. Follow through with his training daily. That's difficult for working moms outside of the home, but it's doable. Hang in there. He won't be in diapers forever.

16. Teach him to pray early, and watch what happens.

When my son Jeff was four years old, he prayed his first heartfelt prayer, which went something like this: "Jesus, help my brother and me to have good dreams, and help the poor people to have pickles." Jeff recited that prayer nightly, which I noted in his baby book. (See Tip 7.) I have no idea where he derived a mental picture of impoverished people starving for Claussen Koshers, but he did.

Every night, my husband and I—stifling smiles and chuckles—would kneel with Jeff at his bedside while he, with head bowed and tiny hands clenched together, interceded on behalf of the needy to receive their fill of baby dills.

One never knows what will slip out of a small boy's psyche. That's part of the adventurous and fun world of sons. Moms, pray aloud for your son beginning at birth. Pray for his boo-boos and his lost stuffed dinosaur. Pray for him before he participates in sports or a school play. Pray at mealtime, bedtime, and all the times in between. Through your daily example, demonstrate how prayer is simply talking to God. A mother's prayers are powerful because no one will pray for your son as fervently, consistently, and frequently as you do.

During my son Jeff's early years, my husband and I conducted a Bible study that met weekly in our home. Bibles open, we talked about life in relationship to the scriptures. Following the study, we'd pray aloud for the prayer requests of others within and outside of the group.

When my son grew older, he often expressed how he, from his bedroom, would hear us praying. Thus, he learned to pray not only from listening to his dad and me, but from hearing a group of Christians interceding for their families and others. Today, he leads prayer in his own home and is typically the one who prays and leads devotions at family functions.

Pray with and for your little ones from the very beginning. Teach them to talk to God about whatever is on their little hearts and minds. They'll surprise you with their special, and often unusual, prayer requests. What's more, God hears and answers their prayers. After all, somewhere in the world, needy people received their fair share of pickles.

A WORD FROM THE WORD:

At that time Jesus prayed this prayer: "O Father, Lord of heaven and earth, thank you for hiding these things from those who think themselves wise and clever, and for revealing them to the childlike."
MATTHEW 11:25 NLT

Think About It . . .

♡ Do you pray for your son in his presence? Why not pray for and with him before he leaves for preschool? If he's worried about a visit to the dentist's or doctor's office, pray first. Doing so instills in him the practice of prayer.

♡ Ask your son to join you in prayer. If he's too shy to pray on his own (and he may be at first), ask if he has any prayer requests he'd like to share. Then pray about them.

♡ Your son will follow your example. If he sees or hears you praying regularly, he will, too. Even if you don't see or hear him, believe it, he's talking to God.

FINAL THOUGHTS:

As your son begins to pray aloud, brace yourself to keep your composure. Some of his heartfelt requests, though serious to him, are humorous to you. If he sees you laugh, it may embarrass him enough to withhold his prayers. One man remembered his childhood prayer. He said: "Dear God, if you can't make me a better boy, don't worry about it. I have a real good time like I am." Can you imagine his mother's reaction? Ah yes, that's a boy for ya!

• •

17. When he is brutally blunt, smile and go with the flow.

• •

"Mommy, is that lady going to have a baby?" your three-year-old son inquires about the overweight woman standing alongside of you at the store.

"Shhh. No, honey," you say in a hushed tone.

"But her tummy looks like she is," he states innocently.

Red-faced, you want to crawl under the counter or, at the very least, pretend he belongs to someone else.

Your son will say what he means and means what he says. No facades for him, although, as the above example shows, his honesty isn't always timely or appreciated.

One little guy ordered "three salted hard-boiled eggs" for his lunch at a family restaurant. The waitress smiled, noting his precision in verbalizing exactly what he wanted.

Waiting until the waitress was out of the boy's earshot but hadn't yet walked away, the boy's mom whispered to the server, "Just two."

When the order arrived, the four-year-old swiftly clarified his intentions. "Thank you," he said as the waitress placed the plate in front of him, "but actually, I wanted three eggs, not two." Excruciatingly honest and polite, but to the point.

The only thing is, your son's comments won't always come across as politeness. His unabashed honesty will embarrass you to no end, especially when he reveals things about you to others that you'd rather keep locked in the home front. Or if he blurts out in public what you told him in private. Small boys know little of social faux pas, so they speak truthfully and freely. So be prepared for just about anything springing from his little lips. And when you correct him, expect a bewildered look as he stares at you with searching eyes and asks more mortifying questions in the presence of everybody.

With age comes filters. That's a good thing. Sometimes. The trade-off is that our childlike innocence is lost in myriad ways as we mature. Unlike our young, through our deliberate silence or insincere nods of agreement, we often find ourselves holding back what we honestly think in order to keep from expressing an opinion that differs from that of mainstream society. So in the name of diplomacy, or desiring acceptance, we dilute our convictions or alter our opinions according to whomever we're with.

Soon your son will withhold his true feelings and battle with being accepted versus holding true to his convictions. But for now he is unpretentious and forthright as he unabashedly expresses himself without apology. So when he's brutally blunt, just go with the flow.

Your son's childlike way mirrors God's way. Jesus was straight forward and uncompromising, yet He epitomized unconditional love and compassion and was eager to minister and forgive. In much the same way, God instructs us to "speak the truth in love" (Ephesians 4:15 NLT). Striking a delicate balance is the key.

Have you ever asked people their opinion and their response was laden with insincere flattery as they tell you what they think you want to hear, rather than the truth? Later you discovered what they really thought. It's impossible to trust folks like that because you are never quite sure of what they really think. They wear facades, false flattery, and insincerity better than supermodels display the latest fashions.

Your son is the salt of the earth. He is honest, innocent, and loving. These are all attributes for which we should strive throughout our lives. Salt is effective because it preserves and flavors. We need more of it, especially on three, not two, hard-boiled eggs.

A WORD FROM THE WORD:

"You are the salt of the earth. But if the salt loses its saltiness, how can it be made salty again? It is no longer good for anything, except to be thrown out and trampled underfoot."
MATTHEW 5:13 NIV

Think About It. . .

- ♡ Most people understand your son's outspokenness. They may even think it's cute, so don't worry about it or become overly concerned.

- ♡ Out of the mouth of babes comes honesty. Help your son develop and maintain honesty balanced with kindness and courtesy.

- ♡ Don't dampen his curiosity. It's part of his learning curve. Silencing him too much sends a mixed message: "Do I tell the truth or not?" Encourage authenticity.

FINAL THOUGHTS:

Want the truth? You'll get it from your toddler. He'll comment about your hair, your dress, or whatever is within his line of sight or touch. He'll remind you of your instructions, expecting you to adhere to them, too. He's curious and will ask people questions like, "Is that a wig or your real hair?" You are mortified, while he's unflappable. As the familiar axiom goes, "The truth hurts." But spoken from your little guy, it may also humiliate—you, not him!

18. Take note: What irritates you today will bless you tomorrow.

Boys are a blessing, no doubt about it. At the same time, they can aggravate us to no end. Does your son get into everything?

Angie claimed that her one son was "all boy" from the start. He was more active, much louder, and more mischievous than her other son. The mischief maker would interrupt her constantly and enter the forbidden areas of her home whenever he had the chance. He drove her crazy with his jumping, running, and hurling himself onto the couch like a rocket propelling off the launching pad.

One day after he had grown, she discovered a shoebox in the storage area beneath her staircase. Immediately, she recognized it as the box in which she kept her high school keepsakes. She'd forgotten that the box even existed after so many years. Eagerly, she swept her hand across its dusty lid to reveal its contents.

She read the school newspaper clippings in which her name was mentioned and scanned prom favors and other memorabilia. Then she noticed something shocking. Each photo in the box was sliced down the middle. *Who could have done this?* The bizarre mystery unfolded when, at the bottom of the box, she found the evidence left behind: A tiny pair of blunt-end scissors. Suddenly it occurred to her that one of her two sons had been the culprit many years prior.

Hmm. Looks like the handiwork of son Todd, she mused. She could visualize chubby-cheeked Todd with his mischievous smile and Dutch boy haircut, viewing her box of treasures as an excellent proving ground for his new child-friendly scissors. Photos, after all, are easy to cut, and isn't that what scissors are for?

Angie held the sliced photos in her hand and thought about how different her reaction would have been had she found the box fifteen years earlier when her then four-year-old son had committed the unseen crime. But finding them years later, long after her son swapped blunt-end scissors for a college notebook, made the discovery endearing and nostalgic. Time makes all the difference.

Greek historian Plutarch said, "Time is the wisest of all counselors." What would have sent that mom into a rage yesterday, amused her today. Matters that once rattled her had lost their punch with the passing of time.

At times you may feel as if your toddler or young son will drive you crazy. A culmination of various aggravations wears you thin so that the slightest indiscretion on your son's part tosses you into a frenzy. That's normal.

We grow as our sons do. Our outlook changes with time, and it is often years before we see the insignificance in the once significant. What you currently deem destructive will evolve into cherished, heartwarming memories.

After Angie finished touring her past, she placed the scissors atop the stack of mementos in a time-honored fashion. Her box of treasures was more priceless than it had been before her little bandit invaded it fifteen years before.

Angie's perspective had changed over the years, and she realized what a blessing her once-little bundle of energy really was. So rest assured, what makes you tug at your hair now about your little guy will bless you in the future.

A WORD FROM THE WORD:

Then, as I looked and thought about it, I learned this lesson.
PROVERBS 24:32 NLT

Think About It. . .

♡ People never stop learning valuable life lessons. Your little son is teaching you right now through his actions and reactions. And you learn as you act or react to him.

♡ Is it hard to imagine that you could ever laugh about melted chocolate covering your living room chair or your son using your guest towels to play tug-of-war with his puppy? Some day you will, but for now take one day at a time. Try to learn from your son's mistakes and the mistakes you are sure to make as his mom. You never stop growing.

FINAL THOUGHTS:

Anais Nin said, "We don't see things as they are, we see them as we are." Viewing your son through a microscope of perfection is unrealistic. That's because a little boy, whose exploratory nature *will* get him into trouble time and time again, is infamous for doing the unexpected and unlikely. How you view his antics will determine how you handle him. Yet, in the end, you will realize your boy is a blessing beyond measure. It just doesn't seem that way as he's tearing through the house, using spatulas and yardsticks as swords.

19. After you hold him, mold him.

That baby of yours is growing. Fast. The holding phase slips by easier than a bar of soap slips from a fisted hand. Then your son enters the molding stage, which is probably the longest and most tedious, yet rewarding, time in a mother's life.

As we teach him about the Savior, we hope to mold our boy into a godly, responsible man. Good character, sound judgment, integrity, courage, and respect are only a few of the attributes we hope to instill in him.

Call on the Lord often for help and wisdom to mold your son during his formative years for, as Jesus said, "Without me you can do nothing" (John 15:5 NKJV). Every mom knows how true those words are.

Little boys are eager beavers. They dash from one object to another. They press their noses against window panes, then finger paint the excess saliva and nose fluid (ick!) all over the glass. They hold lots of surprises, from playing with their poop and licking the dog to bolting through the house in reckless abandon, buck naked.

It's never too early to introduce your son to Jesus through prayer, picture books, and children's videos. While you're at it, teaching him manners is a good thing, too, but don't expect much from a toddler other than getting him to respond with the obligatory "please" and "thank you"—great accomplishments for him. Otherwise, picking his nose in public, adjusting his private parts, and chattering or screaming endlessly to drown out those around him are issues with which to deal as you go along.

Most of all, remember that the molding stage takes years. Your prayers are mandatory, because as you lift him (and yourself) to God, He will direct your path and help keep you sane at the same time. He will provide you with the wisdom you need in any and all situations. There may be times that you fail. That's okay. You will learn from your mistakes as well as your son's.

Evangelist Billy Graham said, "Only God Himself fully appreciates the influence of a Christian mother in the molding of character in her children." The Lord knows what it takes to mold children; after all, He is the most experienced at that task!

Every mom wants her son to become a godly man, devoted to Jesus and His Word. Moms have the distinct privilege and responsibility to influence their sons for God's kingdom.

Molding our son is a call to sacrifice and commitment. We have approximately eighteen years to shape his character—to help him form values. Only through Christ can we consistently correct, admonish, love, and train him in the ways of the Lord. We merely need to remember that such training takes patience, perseverance, spurts of creativity, and a whopping sense of humor. (Remember that the next time your toddler pulls down his pants in public!)

A WORD FROM THE WORD:

Start children off on the way they should go,
and even when they are old they will not turn from it.
PROVERBS 22:6 NIV

Think About It. . .

- 💜 A question to consider: You would lay down your life for your son, but will you lay down your magazine or iPad to consistently correct him or monitor his TV programs?

- 💜 Molding is a call to sacrifice. Paul said to the Philippian church: "But even if I am being poured out like a drink offering. . .I am glad and rejoice with all of you" (Philippians 2:17 NIV). Paul became a living sacrifice for his spiritual children because he knew it would deepen their faith. Not so different from moms.

♡ Think of some ways you can positively mold your son into a godly man of character. Have frequent discussions with your husband about your joint views about raising him.

FINAL THOUGHTS:

Did you ever try to mold a lump of clay on a potter's wheel? As the wheel turns, it's necessary to move your hands in the correct manner with precision and care; otherwise, the lump stays a lump. God molds each person daily, shaping each individual into the person He has envisioned him or her to be. May you as a mother continue to seek the guidance of the Master Potter who will guide your hands as you endeavor to shape your own little jar of clay.

20. Dirt won't hurt.

Accept it, Mom. Boys and dirt are synonymous. We struggle, argue, and even plead with our sons to remain as fresh, clean, and tidy as they were before they left our presence, but it will do little good. That's because in the eyes of little boys, a dirt hill is for climbing and a rain puddle is an invitation to stomp and splash. New jeans are designed to showcase grass-stained slides into home base or tumbles and tackles in football.

For most of our adult lives we moms sweep, dust, and wipe up dirt daily. "Take your shoes off!" we bellow as we hear our son enter the house from an afternoon of baseball practice. "Wash your hands," we remind him before he lifts food to mouth with germy fingers. And they pocket sandy rocks like gold doubloons. Despite all of our efforts, instructions, and pleas, boys are dirt magnets. Worse yet, they don't seem to mind or even notice.

We teach and instruct our sons the importance of cleanliness; however, the old adage that "cleanliness is next to godliness" is (*yikes!*) untrue. Dirt won't hurt, although it will leave most of us in a tizzy and some of us in a perpetual cleaning frenzy.

Face it: Dirt comes with the territory of having sons, just as scraped knees, bloody noses, and yes, an occasional blackened eye does. Although we should and do teach them personal hygiene and cleanliness, what's going on *inside* them is far more important than their outward appearance.

The scriptures instruct us to focus on the more important issues of raising a son, like teaching them the Word of God to build inner character and strength. Salvation and baptism cleanse our son's soul to a gleaming, spiritually bleached-soaked whiteness!

Knowing our son knows Jesus and is living according to God's principles is what really matters. So put away the broom and dust off the Bible. Ditch the dirt from the inside and worry less about the outside.

A WORD FROM THE WORD:

And that water is a picture of baptism, which now saves you, not by removing dirt from your body, but as a response to God from a clean conscience.
1 PETER 3:21 NLT

Think About It. . .

- ♡ God's Word cleanses the heart. When was the last time you opened and read the Bible with your son? Whether he is a toddler or a teen, it's never too early or too late to share God's Word with him.

- ♡ Today, spend less time cleaning and more time interacting with your son. Schedule time each week to put off chores and get down and dirty playing with him.

- ♡ What occupies your thoughts more: Your son's spiritual growth? Or what's growing beneath his bed?

FINAL THOUGHTS:

Moms are multitaskers. Most days they feel as if the burden of the world lies on their shoulders. If moms don't clean up their family's messes, who will? The answer is simple. Solicit your son to help with daily chores. (See Tip 25.) Instruct and guide him on how to clean up his own messes. Set rules, but don't sweat the small stuff. Your son won't die of dirt, but he may die spiritually of a soiled, unrepentant heart.

● ●

21. Believe he'll live up to his name because he will. . .eventually.

● ●

Shakespeare once asked, "What's in a name?" Scripturally speaking, names are significant. For in Bible times, a name designated the individuality of a person; it signified his or her true character.

Carol never gave that much thought until the day her then five-year-old son accompanied her for a day-long excursion to the mall. Rambunctious and inquisitive, Jeffy was her usual handful. He squirmed and whined whenever she shopped too long in one place. Despite her correction, he touched everything in sight, and the moment she turned her back, he promptly grabbed things of interest.

This kid is going to drive me crazy, she grumbled inwardly. *Why did I think I could get any real shopping done with him along?* Frustrated and tired, she decided to forego shopping and head for home. But on her way out of the mall, she made one more stop at a Christian bookstore. On the counter was a display of laminated pocket cards. Arranged in alphabetical order, the cards had proper names with their definitions.

Although her son impatiently tugged at her sleeve, her curiosity prompted her to search for names of family members and friends. Carol: "Song" the card read. *Well, I do love to sing,* she thought. Justin: "Just." *Man! That's true of both my husband and my oldest son.* Jeff: "Divinely Peaceful." *Divinely what? Peaceful? You've got to be kidding.* That one was a mystery.

By now, Jeffy's fussing turned to whimpers: "Come on, Mommy, let's go!"

Hurriedly, she placed the cards back, grabbed her son's hand, and headed for the door. But the two words she scoffed at earlier grabbed her heart. *Lord,* she prayed, *Jeffy is far from peaceful. How can he be so unlike his name?*

What seemed like minutes later, the Lord revealed something she had forgotten. God viewed her ornery, overactive son much differently than she did. He saw Jeffy not as he was, but as he would be.

Right now it's hard to imagine that your little bundle of energy will emerge into a godly gentleman. But with time, prayer, discipline, and love, he will.

Though each of us may fall short of our given names, Jesus views us not as we were or as we are, but who we will become through His power and grace. When we do our part in parenting, God does the rest, and then we all become true to our names—Christians: "Followers of Jesus Christ."

A WORD FROM THE WORD:

The nations will see your righteousness. World leaders will be blinded by your glory. And you will be given a new name by the Lord's own mouth.
ISAIAH 62:2 NLT

Think About It. . .

- ♥ When your son gets on your last nerve, pray for the Lord to help you to view him through His eyes. God's view is clear and will give you a new perspective.

- ♥ It's not your son's given name that's important but the name he makes for himself as he matures. When you underscore your son's strengths, accept and work with his weaknesses, and instill godly principles in his upbringing, you can trust that he will become all that God desired.

- ♥ Teach your son early that a good reputation is an important and noble characteristic. Encourage him to protect his good name.

Throughout the scriptures, God reminds us that He sees people much differently than we do. Good thing! Gideon trembled in fear hiding behind a winepress when the angel of the Lord first named him a "mighty man of valor" (Judges 6:12 NKJV). And, in the end, Gideon lived up to his name.

22. Let him roughhouse; it's a boy thing.

"I never noticed how overactive and daring boys were until I had my son," one mom confessed. "Having two girls, I went into culture shock when I had my son. His rough-and-tumble ways concerned and exhausted me! Now I understand it's just part of a boy's nature."

Boys play hard. They push the limits to their mom's chagrin (and horror). To boys, sticks are great swords, and furniture is meant to be scaled like mountain goats.

One mom was convinced that her son bounced out at birth. Afterward, he could—and would—squeeze into every crevice as he tumbled, twirled, jumped, and hurled nonstop. He outwitted every child-proof safety device in the house as his mom watched him scale the security gate with ease. Sound similar?

A boy dislikes being corralled; it dampens his desire to run and explore. So roughhousing with his dad is normal, even good for him. It's a father-son bonding, a rite of passage like some strange tribal ritual. Though unsettling to dad's female counterpart (who is always standing somewhere nearby hoping no one gets hurt), she needs to simply take a deep breath, walk away, and allow "the boys" to bond.

Along with roughhousing, boys love adventures. My once elementary-age sons used to love a game we devised whenever I drove in unfamiliar surroundings. They would tell me where to turn until we got lost. They savored the uncertainty of it all, though I have to admit I was frightened more than once during one of our "lost" adventures. Yet the game's intrigue and the opportunity for them to explore thrilled them.

"Mom, do you know where we are?" they'd inquire eagerly.

"No, I honestly don't," I'd admit, biting my lower lip as cheers erupted from the confines of our car.

"We're lost!" they'd shout in jubilation.

Maybe that's why father-son expeditions are so appealing and exciting to boys—because they take controlled risks together. Boys gravitate toward roller coasters, action-video games, physical contact sports, and superhero role-playing. Rather than suppressing their desire to engage in horseplay, let them. That's the way God made boys, and although some of their male inclinations are foreign and unsettling to us, it helps them grow, learn, bond, and have fun at the same time.

While your son's antics may drive you crazy, if channeled in the right direction, his ingenuity, energy, and zest for life will serve him well. In the long run, what we deem negative, the Lord sees as potential. Your exploratory, curious, roughhousing son might just become a professional football player someday or, better yet, an explorer, an inventor, or a scientist. So let him loose!

A WORD FROM THE WORD:

This is what the Lord Almighty says. . . "The city streets will be filled with boys and girls playing there."
ZECHARIAH 8:4–5 NIV

Think About It. . .

♡ Dare to explore with your son. Put aside your cautious nature and do something unexpected and exciting. Drive go-carts together. Play miniature golf. Hit baseballs at the batting cage. Run and bike together.

♡ Is there something your son has been asking you to do that you've put off because it's not your thing? Take the plunge and do it.

♡ Have you wondered if something is wrong with your son because he's so active? Relax. In most cases he's just a normal boy. Engage him in something interesting like building Legos or a model airplane. Play tag with him, or take him to the park where he can expend some of his pent-up energy.

FINAL THOUGHTS:

Horseplay is just that. . .play. So relax, Mom. Realizing how females differ from the males of the species helps you to become a better mom to your son—because you're able to accept and meet him where he is, just as God accepts and meets you where you are.

• •

23. Please teach him good manners. Thank you.

• •

Boys are notorious for bad manners. They expel gas and laugh hysterically. They pick their noses in public, and some little tykes (according to firsthand reports from grossed-out girls) have been known to place forefinger to mouth afterward. Okay, let's now attempt to erase that nasty image. Better? My point is that manners rarely come naturally to boys. Moms must teach them consistently with much diligence.

The lessons begin as early as possible. Consider a few essentials. We teach our toddler to say "please" and "thank you" as soon as he is able to talk. Then we instruct him not to interrupt adults while they're talking, unless it's an emergency. If he needs your attention he might say, "Excuse me, Mom."

Asking for permission is a must; otherwise, you might find out later that your son thought it was perfectly fine to bicycle on the open highway ten miles to his friend's house. In the category of permission also comes the knock-when-a-bedroom-door-is-closed rule. This safety feature is mandatory gaining entrance to his parent's bedroom and those of his siblings. It also keeps privacy and modesty in check should a lock be absent on the bathroom door.

Table manners are in a class of their own. How many times have you asked your son to not slurp his soup, grab food, or put his face so close to the plate that his food and face become one? A boy's caveman instincts to eat like a ravenous bear, especially as he reaches puberty (see Tip 55), are likely to raise more than an eyebrow in public. Teaching him how to use utensils begins as soon as he is able to navigate a baby spoon. Picking up food with his fingers is normal for toddlers, but when your eight-year-old son starts forklifting his mashed potatoes with his fingers, it's time to attempt a table-manners intervention.

Of course, every mom tries to limit her son's daily outbursts of hardy burps and gas explosions, primarily in public and *especially* at the dinner table. And whenever he coughs or sneezes, she tries to teach him to cover his mouth, preferably with his shirt sleeve, with which he is familiar since he uses his sleeve frequently as a handy napkin or tissue.

Manners, however, boil down to one word: *consideration*. As we teach our sons good manners, we instill in them consideration for others, beginning in our own household. The mother of etiquette, Emily Post, said it this way: "Manners are a sensitive awareness of the feelings of others. If you have that awareness, you have good manners, no matter what fork you use."

Excuse me, but that's good advice.

A WORD FROM THE WORD:

Even children are known by the way they act,
whether their conduct is pure, and whether it is right.
PROVERBS 20:11 NLT

Think About It. . .

♡ Does your son open the door for you or for older ladies? Even a seven-year-old can learn to open a door for his mom. Early on, one husband taught his two boys to open doors for their mom. It became such a habit that she would automatically wait at a door to allow her husband or one of her sons to open it for her. In doing so, she taught them respect and consideration for girls.

♡ Make it clear that manners aren't optional; they're mandatory.

♡ Ask your son what he thinks good manners are. Make a list and play a game to see how many he can implement during the day.

♡ Name-calling is common with boys but unacceptable. When he resorts to calling his brother a "jerk" or "idiot" or his sister a "snotty-brat," tell him how much names hurt and insist he apologize.

FINAL THOUGHTS:

The development of your son's social graces will carry throughout his lifetime. Today his social skills will be used in the classroom, on the playing field, and in interaction with his peers. Later on, his good manners will serve him well on the job and in society. Teach your son decorum, and you are teaching him how to treat people fairly, with consideration and courtesy.

• •

24. He's unpredictable, so learn what makes him tick.

• •

James Thurber wrote: "Boys are beyond the range of anybody's sure understanding, at least when they are between the ages of eighteen months and ninety years."

One day, your son wows you with his brilliance. The next moment he frustrates you with blatant stupidity. You commend him when he defends his sister, then correct him when he aggravates and teases her minutes later. He'll show compassion for a wounded bird, then suddenly become a bird of a different feather when his brother needs understanding.

Your son is adventurous, fun-loving, caring, annoying, exasperating, intelligent, kind, rude, loving, and difficult—all rolled up into one unpredictable package. One moment he'll alarm you with is recklessness and annoy you with his behavior, and then charm you with his wit and endearing manner the next.

So rather than sequestering yourself in a corner to babble to yourself and wring your hands, think stability. Yours. Act, don't react, to his unpredictability, although that's far easier said than done. A mom's first reaction is to react. You're tired, frustrated, and you've had a long day. But when your son smacks his sibling, discipline, don't scream.

Stand resolute in the idea that this, too, shall pass. Your son won't always hang out his bedroom window like Spiderman, and he'll outgrow his habit of appearing in the living room (in front of guests) with pants down to his knees in a silent plea for you to pull them up after a bathroom session. (Although, I don't know if boys ever outgrow hosing the toilet seat. See Tip 15.)

As we learn more about our sons and what makes them tick, kick, run amok, dare, and double-dare, we can relax into a mode of stability about their unpredictability. God will and does provide wisdom to raise our sons to become all that He intended. So go with the flow as best you can, and administer the love, discipline, direction, and stability he sorely needs.

A WORD FROM THE WORD:

Don't act thoughtlessly, but understand what the Lord wants you to do.
EPHESIANS 5:17 NLT

Think About It. . .

♡ In frustration, have you ever prayed, "Lord, what in the world should I do with this kid?" You're a mom among many. Boys need guidelines and structure. Knowing what to expect or what's expected of him makes life a little easier for both of you. Set basic rules to follow: No jumping on the furniture; no hitting; no hanging from the chandelier, and so on.

♡ Boys act on a whim, but you act with purpose. He requires structure, and you're the one who can provide that.

FINAL THOUGHTS:

Your son doesn't mean to frustrate you. He doesn't purposely plan to drive you crazy or test your patience. It just happens. Choose your battles. Address what's relevant, necessary, and important to address, and release the rest (at least for the moment).

• •

25. Help him help you—assign chores.

• •

To most boys, chores are a bore; unless, of course, you catch them at an early age. Little boys are mommy's helpers. Ask your four-year-old to give you a hand, and he eagerly uses his boy-generated enthusiasm to help you vacuum or Windex the windows. Granted, he might use the vacuum as a power tool and may get carried away with the spray bottle, leaving your windows wet with long strokes of streaked fingerprints, but he has a heart to help.

Enjoy that phase while you can, because as he grows he begins to grumble at the mere mention of that dreaded word, *chores*. "Clean your room," you tell him, only to find him hours later sitting on the floor, fiddling with a toy. "Take out the trash," you instruct, to which he responds, "In a minute, Mom." The following morning, you enter the kitchen and the smell of rotting garabage overwhelms you.

Becky, mother of Jack, said that after reprimanding her then nine-year-old son to clean his room, pick up his toys, brush his teeth and hair, and other reasonable motherly requests, he gazed up at her with his big brown eyes and boldly proclaimed, "But Mom, I just want to have fun!"

Boys just want to have fun! Forget chores, hygiene, and other such nonsensical attempts at cleanliness. Your son wants to enjoy being a smelly, unkempt, free-spirited, overactive, no-holds-barred boy. So how do we help him help out?

Boys are men in the making. God designed them to lead, provide, and protect. Draw from his innate masculine sensibilities to help take the chore out of chores. "Honey, could you help me today?" you ask.

"What, Mom?" he replies.

"Well, I need you to help me rake leaves." Warning: This may *not* work in all instances. But typically your son will step in to assist his mom-in-need.

In order to prepare our sons for adulthood, marriage, and parenthood, we need to begin training them while they're at home. Encourage him to help around the house to teach him responsibility and the rewards of earnest, hard work. Talk to your spouse about providing an allowance as an incentive, if that's what you decide. Regardless, age-appropriate chorse are a must in every household to promote solid work habits and teamwork. Engage your son in painting a room, carrying in the groceries, and using power tools under the supervision of his dad or another experienced male family member. When your boy is the appropriate age, invite him to help you cook or teach him how to cut vegetables. (See Tip 41.) Then praise him for his efforts and accomplishments.

Make a list of chores for him to manage. Begin with taking out the trash and mowing the lawn. As he gets older, add doing his own laundry (although that one somehow fails to marshal his masculine sensibilities!).

A few notes about laundry: It's achievable, but brace yourself for some major mishaps. Prepare to grimace when he trots off to school in the same jeans and T-shirt two days in a row because all of his clothes are dirty. And don't wait until he's one month away from college to help him navigate separating whites from the darks. By then, he may claim he's color blind!

A WORD FROM THE WORD:

Good planning and hard work lead to prosperity,
but hasty shortcuts lead to poverty.
PROVERBS 21:5 NLT

Think About It. . .

- ♡ God frowns on laziness and rewards hard work. If you teach your son those principles early on, you give him a jumpstart on becoming an adult male equipped and eager to work hard, live right, and provide for his family.

- ♡ Do you tend to do everything yourself rather than solicit the help of your son? It's easier to manage most tasks ourselves rather than laboriously barrage our son with instructions. But asking him for help now will pay off in the long run. So be sure to tell him what to do, and allow him to make mistakes. That's how he'll learn and eventually get it right.

- ♡ Make a list of chores your son could easily manage. Sit down as a family and go over the list. Compromise and provide alternative chores for those he absolutely hates to do.

FINAL THOUGHTS:

The Bible states that there is a time for everything. There's a time for fun and a time for work. Chores are work, and boys need to learn the benefits and satisfaction of giving their best effort. The scriptures instruct us that whatever work we do, do it to the best of our ability (see Ecclesiastes 9:10). Convey that biblical principle to your son through personal example and give him responsibility for household duties. His future wife will thank you for it!

· ·

26. Allow his imagination to go wild. . . because it will anyway.

· ·

"Batman to the rescue!" Alex yells as he runs through the house, one end of a throw blanket tucked into his back collar. The caped crusader whizzes past you, arms extended as the blanket flaps in the air.

Young boys are creative and innovative. We see a serving spoon, they see a sword; we see bunk beds, they see a jungle gym; we see an area rug, they see a flying carpet; we see a chair, they see the cockpit of an airplane; we see a large cardboard box with empty paper towel rolls shoved through crudely cut holes, they see a fort with cannons or telescopes shoved through its portals.

Just watch a small boy at Christmas. Did you ever go through the time and trouble to buy your son the gifts he wanted, only to watch him open the presents, toss the contents aside, and start playing with the box?

Boys play fireman complete with corresponding siren sounds, using anything with wheels. Rocks fascinate our sons, as do crawling things. Some boys collect both with much pride and satisfaction.

After a day of outside play, he smells like wet puppies. During bath time, he transitions from land-action superhero to under-the-sea explorer complete with face mask and plunging vessels. If a toy boat is unavailable, no problem. A soap dish will do.

These are normal traits with which boys are born. Commentator George Will said: "Some parents say it is toy guns that make boys warlike. But give a boy a rubber duck and he will seize its neck like the butt of a pistol and shout 'Bang!' "

Get used to it. Your son is the inventor of raucous play. He plays hard, complete with corresponding voice-activated sounds and noise. So let him. One man said of his dad, "My father used to play with my brother and me in the yard. Mother would come out and say, 'You're tearing up the grass.' 'We're not raising grass,' Dad would reply. 'We're raising boys.' " That smart dad had it right. Enjoy, encourage, and even partake in your son's playfulness (if you can muster the energy).

Boys and imagination go together like burping and babies. They must explore and pretend; it is part of their nature and integral to their development. Or as author Johann Christoph Arnold wrote: "It is a beautiful thing to see a child thoroughly absorbed in his play; in fact, it is hard to think of a purer, more spiritual activity."

Allowing your son's imagination to run wild stimulates his brain while expending some pent-up energy at the same time. Now that's a winning combination. As the renowned physicist of the twentieth century, Albert Einstein, said: "Imagination is more important than knowledge." Wow, imagine that!

Think About It. . .

♡ Whether or not you believe it, your son's imagination comes from God. He has engineered your little boy's growing brain to think, create, and imagine wonderful, exciting things.

♡ Enjoy his fun, spirited side. As you notice him switching into high-gear, join him. Share jokes, laugh, and engage in child's play.

♡ If your son asks you to role-play, join him. He'll rescue you from evildoers and defend you from harm—good precursors to the real world that lies beyond his spooned sword.

FINAL THOUGHTS:

Your God is a God of creativity. He imagined the world and its inhabitants long before He spoke them into existence. Likewise, He gifts your son with an imagination and play, the experience of which can later be used for His glory. Under the influence of the Holy Spirit, your boy's imagination grows and matures into creating and accomplishing great things for the kingdom of God. And to think it all started with a makeshift Batman cape.

• •

27. Respect your son's dad.

• •

Okay, so you're painfully aware of your husband's shortcomings and idiosyncrasies. In fact, he often gets on your last nerve. In general, men don't get it. He asks you where you put the bug spray, you give him explicit directions and—though the can stares him square in the face—he doesn't see it.

"I can't find it!" he yells through the house, while you're knee-deep in another project. "Where'd you say it was?"

Ugh! "I said it's in the utility room's upper right-hand cabinet on the first shelf!" A few minutes pass.

"It's not there!"

So you leave what you're doing, tromp through the house to pick up the spray can that's directly in front of his nose, and hand it to him.

"Oh, I didn't see it," he says as you walk away, totally bugged about him and his bug spray. Sound familiar?

Men's mental patterns differ from ours in *so* many ways! But the truth is, we aggravate them with our feminine proclivities just as much as they annoy us with theirs. It is said that boys have approximately a thirty-second attention span. Men's attention spans aren't too far off from that. Males tend to focus intently on the things that interest them the most. (Locating the bug spray is not one of them. Neither is listening to every morsel of verbal trivia we express.)

By nature men are hunters, providers, and protectors. They excel at problem solving and logic. They are goal oriented and they value achievement. At times, your other half will seem cold and—in your estimation—lack compassion for your son's personal dilemmas. He will handle your son's situations the opposite of how you would deal with them. This can—and often does—cause conflict. The last thing you need while raising sons, or children in general, is disagreement between you and your spouse about their upbringing. Presenting a united front is paramount, even if you disagree on some things.

Contrary to society's politically correct claims, God has hardwired men and women differently for good reason—to fulfill our individual roles in our marriage, family, and life. He meant for us to complement one another. Where one leaves off, the other takes over. When our emotions run away with us, our husband's logic brings calm and clarity.

As you respect and *show* respect for your husband, you set a positive example for your son to witness—namely, that mom not only loves dad, she respects and honors him. Your son then begins to understand his own place in this world and will embrace the natural, God-given attributes of a godly man: strength, character, competence, leadership, bravery, wisdom, and integrity.

Do your son a favor; respect your husband. Even when he can't find the bug spray.

Think About It. . .

- ♡ Can you think of ways to show your husband respect? Do you tell him how much you admire him? Do so in the presence of your son.

- ♡ Do you expect, require, and teach your son to show his dad (and you) respect?

- ♡ Your husband has much to offer, so solicit his advice, suggestions, input, and direction often. His perspective will help you to gain a better handle on mothering your son.

- ♡ Consider all the ways your husband provides for you and your family. List his attributes and it won't take you long to appreciate him deeply. Tell him how much you love him.

FINAL THOUGHTS:

Women need to feel loved and understood. Men crave respect and admiration. No, they aren't on an ego trip—it's the way God made them. When you understand and embrace that fact, you will respect your husband out of respect for your God.

28. Teach him that giving isn't seasonal, even though it seems like it.

Is giving a natural instinct? Ever observe your son or someone else's child at play? Often they're refreshingly willing to share a toy. If the child is yours, you breathe a sigh of relief and prematurely administer yourself a pat on the back. But most of the time, sharing or not sharing a prized possession, or anything else for that matter, turns into a battle of the wills complete with shoving, crying, whining, and, well, you've been there.

These are your son's formative years: A time of learning and growing like none other. Now is the time to instill in him the act of giving. Your example and instruction will either stick with him like a tongue on frozen metal, or slip through his psyche like a boy sledding down an icy snow hill.

Here's how it went down in my family when my two sons were growing up. Every Christmas, a surge of generosity and sentiments of peace-on-earth-good-will-toward-men overtook me. It was as if an angel descended from heaven, sprinkling good-intention dust all over me. Like magic, I found myself enthralled in a search for humanitarian deeds to do.

The upcoming Christmas season meant it was time to venture out on a buying expedition to purchase groceries and gifts for a local needy family from our church. The boys would add their saved dollars to ours and we'd choose age-appropriate toys and clothing. Just before the holiday, the four of us would march up to the family's doorstep to present our tokens of love and good cheer.

Returning home, a sense of righteous self-satisfaction settled in our hearts. We felt great. We were now free to return home to our Christmas celebrations with gifts and goodies, void of guilt. After all, we had done our part while teaching our children the joy of giving at the same time. Right?

However, one Christmas I came to a startling and sobering revelation. It happened while my husband and I discussed what our Christmas contribution would be that year. "Why don't we look into serving meals at the Salvation Army?" I suggested.

"Sounds great," he replied, "Maybe the kids could help, too."

What a wonderful family experience, I thought. *This is better than anything we have done before. Imagine, actually treading on their turf to provide the homeless and needy with the gift of our time wrapped up in a loving smile.*

Suddenly my self-serving motives rose to the surface. Why were we doing what we were doing? For whom were we doing it? The needy? Or were we actually doing these good deeds for ourselves? If our desire was to help the less fortunate, then why was our generosity displayed only during the holidays or in cases of natural disasters? The poor and needy are poor and in need all year round. Where was our spirit of generosity the rest of the year?

That startling observation taught me a valuable lesson that I passed on to my sons. Giving is a way of life, not a part-time act of service to relieve guilt. Boys aren't as innately tuned into the needs of others as girls are. So teaching your sons to give begins early so that, hopefully, they carry a giving attitude and spirit with them throughout their lifetimes. The search for humanitarian deeds to do is not exclusive to the Christmas season or any other holiday. So much for good-intention angel dust!

A WORD FROM THE WORD:

"For I was hungry and you gave me something to eat, I was thirsty and you gave me something to drink, I was a stranger and you invited me in, I needed clothes and you clothed me. . . . Whatever you did for one of the least of these brothers and sisters of mine, you did for me."
MATTHEW 25:35–36, 40 NIV

Think About It. . .

♡ Can you think of ways you teach your son to give? Jot them down. If you find yourself lacking, think of things you can do to implement a spirit of giving in your home.

♡ Giving entails much more than writing a check, although that's needed, too. Do you exemplify a giving spirit in your daily life? For instance: If the person in front of you in the checkout lane is short on some change, do you offer to pay the difference? If an elderly lady struggles to open a door or carry her groceries, are you eager to help her? These are golden opportunities for you to solicit your son's help as well, teaching him to revere and respect the elderly.

♡ When your son receives a gift, have him write a good old-fashioned thank-you note! He will balk and complain at first, and might even insist on sending an email or text instead. Regardless, instill in him the importance of good manners and the act of showing appreciation.

FINAL THOUGHTS:

One quote poses a thought-provoking challenge. It says: "Ask your children two questions this Christmas. First: 'What do you want to give to others for Christmas?' Second: 'What do you want for Christmas?' The first fosters generosity of heart and an outward focus. The second can breed selfishness if not tempered by the first."

The scriptures note that Jesus loves a cheerful giver. Giving is more a matter of the heart than an outward action. As you give and teach your son to give, discuss the blessings of giving from a willing heart.

• •

29. Accept that you are destined to participate in boy activities.

• •

You know how it goes. You shop the action figure and Xbox gaming aisles at toys stores. If you have all boys, as I did, you might pass by the girls' section, eyeing doll houses and Barbie dolls, dreaming of pink in a world of blue. "Oh, isn't that pink frilly tutu darling?" you tell your disinterested husband. "Uh-huh," he mutters, accommodating you.

And so it goes. Disney World offers lots of fun for boys *and* girls. But there will be no Cinderella, Belle, or Ariel the Mermaid for you. You won't attend the Disney tea party or have dinner with princesses atop Cinderella's castle. But you will surely accompany your boys to the Jedi Training Academy and Captain Jack Sparrow's pirate adventure. You'll soar on Space Mountain, race at Tomorrowland Speedway, and raft to Tom Sawyer's Island to visit Injun Joe's Cave. You will meet with Buzz Lightyear and Woody and search for Mater the car. Wherever you vacation, chances are you'll be heading for tourist attractions that sport go-carts, arcade games, and anything else that is loud and fast.

Although it often grates on our feminine nerves, mothering a boy comes with doing what he likes to do. If he likes to fish, we board the dingy and cast a line—or drop the line in the water might be more like it. Although you might get squeamish about baiting the hook, the excitement of actually catching a big—or more realistically a small—fish will delight your son and create lasting memories. Partake in his activities when you can, or are able. Play wiffle ball or shoot hoops with him. Ride roller coasters, if he invites you.

I was never one for going on a ride that would jolt, whip, and rattle my insides. But I would relent occasionally if the ride wasn't too jarring. The summer before my eldest son left for college, we visited a theme park. Both of my sons begged me to join them on the newest and fastest roller coaster at the time. After bantering back and forth, my son hit my mom button when he said, "Come on, Mom, do it for me. I'll be leaving home soon. It'll be fun." I couldn't refuse.

So we reluctantly stood in a long line for what seemed like hours. Finally, our turn came. A padded black safety bar lowered in front of me from the back. By now, my husband and two sons were having a field day, teasing me about the ride. "You know it goes backward," one of them mentioned, *after* it was too late to exit. "You'll be okay, Mom, just hold on tight and close your eyes." Uh-huh. I, not the ride, was now the main attraction of my sons' amusement.

The Dare Devil Dive (the name alone should have clued me in) was the worst amusement-park experience of my life. My head whipped from side to side and bounced back and forth, as my cheeks shook with each jarring move. With eyes squeezed shut, I made moaning screams. This caused my eldest son, who sat next to me, to laugh hysterically during the entire ordeal.

Afterward, I suffered from roller-coaster aftershock. I walked away from the ghastly ride, muttering to myself and hoping my brain would settle back into its skull. To this day, my sons reminisce about the time they convinced me to ride the "Dive" and how I entertained them with my reaction.

Part of parenting is putting aside our preferences to fulfill the desires of our boys. We can and should enter their world to participate in the activities and things they like to do. And although you may suffer from whiplash or worse, God will bless you as He helps you and your son build lasting memories together that neither of you will ever forget (even though you'd like to!).

A WORD FROM THE WORD:

Wherever you go and whatever you do, you will be blessed.
DEUTERONOMY 28:6 NLT

Think About It. . .

♡ When was the last time you did something your son liked to do? Set time aside during the week to do at least one activity with him.

♡ Okay, so you don't know how to play basketball or ride a skateboard. He doesn't care. All your son wants is for you to show enough interest to try it out! He may even teach you a new skill in the process.

♡ Boys are fun, so enter into your son's world. Does he have a favorite place to go? Take him, even if you don't participate.

FINAL THOUGHTS:

If you've grown up with a brother or two, boys may have always been part of your life, and so you learned early how to partake in games and activities that interest the male of the species. On the other hand, you may have come from a family with mostly girls, so having a boy was a culture shock at first. But you also discovered how fun-loving and adventurous boys are. In reckless abandon they attempt things girls would never dream of doing. And there's nothing like a mom who is willing to join them in their play and, yes, even their mischief.

30. Don't nag, negotiate.

"Take your shoes off and set them to the side," you tell your son for the umpteenth time. Nevertheless, you stumble over his clunky high tops the next time you enter the back door.

"Clean your room!" you mandate.

He shoves desktop items into his drawers, kicks dirty socks and underwear beneath his bed, and stuffs his closet with the remainder of debris that litters his room. Then he calls it a day.

You walk in, unimpressed as you notice papers peaking out the top of his desk drawer, underwear amid dust bunnies emerging from beneath his bed, and various sports equipment trying to escape from the closet, the door left ajar. "I told you to clean your room," you flatly state.

"I did, Mom," he replies. "See?"

This scenario, or anything like it, becomes your *aha* moment or your moment of exasperation as you realize that boys think *clean* means "If it's tucked beneath, behind, or out of sight, it's clean." Although we can teach him to dust, vacuum, and organize, getting a son to regularly do such tasks is like trying to lead a horse into a blazing fire.

So in our frustration we begin to nag in an attempt to get our point across. Having had two male children, I, the lone female, was the minority in my family. But I attempted to hang in there with my boys.

My husband and sons loved to tent camp, so I tried it several times, even though the smell of canvas mixed with mosquito repellent exasperated my feminine sensitivities. And wrapped in a musty sleeping bag while lying on a polyethylene floor was about as appealing to me as eating mashed potatoes with a hair in them.

But I endured as I swept out the tent, lit the citronella candle, and set up camp my way—namely, tablecloth and centerpiece, not to mention a throw rug which I positioned at the tent's door. The male trio objected to my domesticating their space, and my husband refused to take off his shoes inside of the tent.

"Mommmm, we're camping!" my sons whined, after I warned them about a swarm of flying insects that were about to enter our tarpaulin abode.

What blew the tent out of the campground was nighttime. After showering in a moth-infested bath house, I returned to the tent to find my male trio crawling into their sacks fully clothed.

"But I brought your pajamas," I protested, but to no avail.

Although I tried to keep my mouth shut and adjust, the strain of trying to appear cheerful while swatting insects, emptying sand from my shoes, and toasting marshmallows on gritty twigs was too much.

So I nagged. A lot. And then the realization finally slapped me in the face like pelting rain. My constant nagging was robbing my macho males of the outdoor experience. As they bonded with nature and each other, I rained bird doo-doo on their campground. It became clear that my interpretation of bonding with nature could only occur inside a thirty-foot Winnebago equipped with full kitchen, bathroom, and beds. So rather than strip my men of their need to sweat, smell, and eat sardines from a can, I decided something had to give. Me.

The scriptures warn women about nagging. With my sniveling remarks, I had started a rainstorm in our camp but stopped thundering when I realized what I had been doing.

Whenever we attempt to fashion our sons to our whims and ways, nagging ensues with motor-mouth consistency. This is where negotiation enters. We can fold our arms and stand our ground, or we can make some allowances and compromise. Boys need to learn obedience, yet at the same time, we need to learn to suppress our nagging and discuss matters with understanding and patience.

So be sure to compromise whenever you can. It'll save you and everyone else a lot of unnecessary stress.

A WORD FROM THE WORD:

A quarrelsome wife [woman] is as annoying
as constant dripping on a rainy day.
PROVERBS 27:15 NLT

Think About It. . .

- ♡ How do you currently handle certain situations in your home? How might you handle things differently?

- ♡ Tell your son what you expect when you ask him to do something, and if he doesn't follow through, enforce some consequences. Be specific. What does "clean your room" mean? Make a chart for your young boy to help him remember his chores. Give your older son a warning: Only two "I forgots" and then consequences.

- ♡ Sit down with your son and discuss where you both need to make changes. Let him voice his thoughts and opinions, and then try to come to a compromise. (Remember, although everything is open for discussion, some things, like following house rules and maintaining godly principles, are nonnegotiable. As long as he is under your roof, your rules rule.)

FINAL THOUGHTS:

Nagging seldom produces results. Instead, it exhausts the nagger herself, aggravates dads, and annoys the kids. It produces disruption and wreaks havoc in your household. Before you know it, your kids are tuning you out. Decide what is really important and what you can let go. Implement a set of rules and expectations for your son to follow. Then help him accomplish them with supportive guidance and instruction. Women often nag from fatigue, feelings of disrespect, lack of support, or when they sense they're losing control. If that's what's happening with you, talk to your husband about it, and see where he can step in to help.

31. Allow him to get hurt even if it pains you.

Ouch! This one stings! From the time our son is small, we protect him. It's our nature to do so.

Did you ever watch a mother bear protecting her young? She has her eye on him at all times, intending to divert any trouble that may arise.

We're much the same as we hover over our son. We rush to break his fall when he's a toddler. We bandage scraped knees. We dread taking our child to the doctor for vaccinations, feeling like we're betraying junior as we hold him down while the physician pokes and prods.

Our feelings don't change much as he gets older. The one difference is that now we have to keep a reasonable distance from him while he face-plants in a football skirmish or receives a spiked shoe to the neck in a soccer game. We stand helplessly on the sidelines, wanting to intervene but standing our ground instead, waiting breathlessly until we see that he's okay.

Our protective nature extends far beyond the physical. We reach fighting mode if our son is treated unfairly, teased, or bullied. We hurt when someone else hurts him. We get tangled in a web of emotions as we observe our son trying to handle difficult situations on his own.

Moms are great comforters and great counselors. Now is the time to protect your son without shielding him completely. Truth is, you couldn't protect him completely even if you tried. That's because, unfortunately, pain—from broken limbs to broken hearts—is inevitable throughout our lifetimes. And how your son learns to manage it now will equip him for the future.

So what can you do to help your son? Consider a few suggestions. If your son falls and hurts himself (and he will), keep calm. If he sees you react, he will unravel all the more. Care for him with calm assurance and comfort, even though you are as frightened as a fox in the hunt.

Teach him early that pain, disappointment, and failure are part of life and will not only pass, but probably help him to learn a valuable life lesson. Let him cry. It's okay! To tell him that "big boys don't cry" is a disservice to him and discriminatory (do we say that to our daughters?). Boys have emotions that they should feel free to express, and crying is one of the ways to express sadness, pain, or disappointment.

Talk him through his pain. Allow him to convey how he feels, even if his perspective is distorted. Give him understanding lathered with loving lessons to learn.

Then let him work through the pain. Don't abandon him, but allow time to pass while giving him loving support. If we overdramatize, he will, too. But as we comfort and assist him through whatever he is experiencing, he'll see that he has an advocate in you, i.e., a strong support system, which is what he really needs anyway.

We don't want our children to hurt. Yet in our attempts to run interference we may often, due to our motherly fears, limit our son by restricting his activities or sports involvement. What we must realize is that there are times that he will fall. Life will deal him some blows. Our job is to allow our son to experience them.

A WORD FROM THE WORD:

Oh, my dear children! I feel as if I'm going through labor pains for you again, and they will continue until Christ is fully developed in your lives.
GALATIANS 4:19 NLT

Think About It. . .

♡ The apostle Paul felt the emotional and spiritual pain of a parent when he wrote the verse above. As a mom, you feel much the same way. You hurt when your boy hurts, and that will continue in different and various forms throughout his and your lifetimes. The good news is that the Holy Spirit is the best Comforter. As you love and comfort your son, so does God, strengthening him with every tear he sheds, every fall he takes.

♡ First Thessalonians 5:17 says to "pray without ceasing" (NKJV). With boys, that's a given! Before every sport's event, pray with him before you leave home. God will protect your son—whatever his age—in better ways than you can. Take comfort in the fact that although at times you may be absent from your son, God is always present.

FINAL THOUGHTS:

Henri Nouwen said, "When we honestly ask ourselves which person in our lives means the most to us, we often find that it is those who, instead of giving advice, solutions, or cures, have chosen rather to share our pain and touch our wounds with a warm and tender hand." You are that warm and tender hand, touching the wounded knee or broken heart of your son. Cushion his pain with the God-given love you have for him.

32. Pace him and his activities.

We live in a fast-paced society and we've made it that way. Shocked? Think about it. Most of us seek the quickest and easiest routes in daily living. We frequent drive-through windows; we opt for faster-speed Internet service; we hate lines or waiting for anything. Advanced technology was intended to make our lives easier and provide us with more time. It accomplished the opposite. We move at record speed, squeezing in a multitude of activities and work-related issues in one day.

Do you have trouble keeping up with your son's schedule? Are you whisking him from one activity to another? Is he overtired and irritable? Are you? Although this might sound like an infomercial for protein bars or instant-success mega vitamins—guaranteed to boost your metabolism and send energy surges through your body like electrical bolts—these are reasonable questions for today's mother of boys.

Every mom wants her son to evolve into a well-rounded individual and live a balanced life complete with responsibility, play, education, spirituality, fun, and challenges. You're focused on your son's interests and help him pursue them. Nothing wrong with that. The problem lies in his overinvolvement that sends him—and you—darting in every direction like a fly that was just dosed with insecticide.

Consider the overactive approach. This is the mom who wants her boy to succeed in whatever he does. Who doesn't, right? So after school three days a week, she takes him for tutoring in math and reading. Two days a week are reserved for church and his youth group involvement. Twice a week, depending on the season, is his basketball, soccer, or baseball practice, and if she can swing it, she takes him to weekly music lessons all year round.

Do the math, and one quickly sees that one week isn't enough time to cover her son's activities. The solution? Double up! Take him to and from one practice, and to and from another activity back-to-back. Then of course there are weekend games galore, followed by end-of-the-season tournaments. In between, he has band practice, does lots of homework, a few (very few) chores, and eats on the run, faster than it takes time to fill next week's calendar. That leaves little time for family and/or fun. What's more, this eager mom tries to keep the pace while juggling everything else that beckons her like a crying baby—and sometimes it is, in fact, a crying baby.

So what's a mother to do? At the risk of sounding like an infomercial again, consider these suggestions:

♡ **Allow your son to choose one after-school activity or sport.** Okay, so your son is a born jock; he excels athletically. He's also one boy with more important things to do than play sports. (Shock!)

♡ **Discuss with your spouse what is too much or just enough involvement**. Come to an agreement and then give your son some options. Cut the unnecessary stuff; limit the other.

♡ **Set priorities**. This is personal. What's of most value to you and your family? Make a list of what you deem most important and least important. Then schedule your son's activities around it.

Stop the runaway railroad and jump off the train. Make your destination a stable environment with reasonable involvement and definitive limits. For your son's sake—as well as your own—reassess your schedules. Pace yourselves and your boy, Mom. Even God took a day of rest. What makes us think that we can keep going?

A WORD FROM THE WORD:

"I have no peace, no quietness;
I have no rest, but only turmoil."
JOB 3:26 NIV

Think About It. . .

♡ Is your son's life too busy? Is yours? Rest is essential for kids and their parents. Create a do-nothing day. Plan nothing. Go nowhere. Stay at home, chill out, and rest.

♡ Does your son love music? Pursue guitar, piano, or whatever instrument that draws his interest. Replace that with something he currently does that he is bored with.

♡ Commit to do something either with your son or as a family once a week. Church doesn't count, since in most places of worship the kids have their own Sunday school classes or youth programs.

♡ Dispel the myth. More isn't necessarily better!

FINAL THOUGHTS:

Make an attempt to stop the fast-paced madness for the next generation. Help your son sort through the plethora of activities in which he participates. Focus on a few, and abandon the others faster than you would a building teetering on collapse. If you don't, you might just collapse next!

Boys, like everyone and everything else in life, are incredibly alike yet distinctively different. Admit it, ladies: In general, we generalize the male gender. Especially when it fits our mood or after our husbands do something so male-like. "Isn't that just like a man?" we assert with arms crossed.

This entire book focuses on the commonalities boys share; yet ask a mom of several sons if all of them are alike and she'll answer with a resounding, "No!"

As the mother of two sons, I would concur. Jimmy is serious, intense, quiet, and a goal-oriented leader. Jeff is outgoing, fun-loving, boisterous, more of a follower, and easy going. Both played sports as kids, but their differences far outweighed their commonalities. The same holds true today.

My three grandsons are completely different, too. Ian, the eldest, has the personality of his uncle Jimmy, though he physically resembles his dad, Jeff. Ian, seventeen, is serious, quiet, and a deep thinker. He loves to read and has been doing so since age four. He's intellectual, disinterested in sports, and is a self-ascribed "nerd." His brother Isaac, thirteen, is outgoing, sensitive, and the sportsman among his three brothers. He is Mr. Personality like his dad. While Alex, seven, is a combination of both of his older brothers: He loves to talk, is a covert intellectual (he's great at hiding just how much he knows and learns), and there's no mistaking his presence in a room.

Yes, every boy is different. If your son doesn't like to play sports, don't force him. Sure, his dad may have been a basketball star, and you were the volleyball queen, but that doesn't mean your son will hold the same interests. The physicians and scientists of our day were nerds as kids. Encourage him to pursue the avenues in which he has interest or talent. If he loves playing sports, allow him to choose several each school year, while encouraging him to hit the books as well.

Treat him as the individual he is. Avoid squeezing him into the stereotypical boy box. God treats and meets us all at our individual levels of growth, experience, talents, weaknesses, and needs. A perceptive mom does the same with her sons.

Think About It. . .

💙 Have you ever pressured your son to become what you wanted him to be? Try this exercise: The next time you are tempted to tell him what you expect, ask him what he expects of himself. What are his aspirations? What does he like or dislike? Help him verbalize those thoughts.

💙 Accentuate your son's strengths and assist him with his weaknesses. Above all, love him through everything.

💙 Support him. A mom is the one person a son looks to for validation. Moms create an atmosphere of acceptance and understanding.

FINAL THOUGHTS:

Your son is special and unique unto himself. Applaud his individuality. After all, you are your son's greatest fan. You sit in the bleachers of his life to support, encourage, and cheer him on. You know your son is special. The Lord has endowed him with gifts and talents that may differ from his siblings. And God wants to use him for His glory. Let him know that, and guide him to that end.

34. Build on the moments of his life, both significant and less so.

The conversation turned reminiscent as we chatted with our son and daughter-in-law one evening.

"I had such a great childhood," Jim confided. "When Robin and I have kids, I hope we will be as good and loving parents as you guys were, and are."

Wow, what mom doesn't long to hear that? In fact, we wait for it practically all of our lives! The reward delivered in our son's words surpassed the most prestigious, sought-after prize a mom could hope to attain, yet alone believe. His remarks soothed an ever-increasing parched and tired mind and body like a cool breeze on a hot, humid day, although I'm convinced that he had forgotten those steamy days when his father and I acted more like tyrants than trustees.

What do you remember about your childhood? Specifics matter, but chances are you recall only the generalities of your home atmosphere and overall care. While adjusting our own parental gauge, we need look no further than our own childhood experiences and ask: What do I want for my son? More importantly, what am I willing to do or sacrifice to achieve that?

In an era when single parenting was atypical, my mom struggled to provide for my two brothers and me. She worked continuously and did her best, but I yearned for the security of a two-parent home that all of my friends enjoyed.

So as a young mom, my solitary goal was to provide my sons with the warm, secure, family atmosphere I never had. Honestly, without Christ in my life, I doubt my son would have shared the sentiment that my husband and I were—and are—good and loving parents.

Truth is, we're all imperfect and flawed. In fact, it's a wonder our sons survive, let alone thrive. Yet our devotion to the Lord motivates us to put our kids first. Their health, safety, and spiritual, emotional, and physical welfare are foremost in our thoughts because of Christ in our lives.

Motherhood requires on-the-job training. There's the new mom, exhausted from little sleep; the mom who wipes sticky hands and spilt milk while she rushes to gather her kids to leave for an outing, school, or church; the overwhelmed mom who manages work and home responsibilities with the strength of a soldier and the organization of a corporate giant; the mom who prays for her estranged-adult child; or the aging mom who peers through her nursing home window, hoping for a visit—all warriors in the lifelong battle to see their child become all that God desires.

Like you and me, not one of those moms is perfect. We pray

for our sons, no matter their ages; we instruct, teach, lead, and trust without evidence of any positive results. We hope that our sons will one day express appreciation; but that's not our driving force. God is. He compels us to become all that we can be, namely, a mom who raises her son in a loving environment and godly home.

Whether or not your son ever expresses appreciation for what you have done, or are doing, is not the goal. Your son is already God's instrument of reward to you. So build on the moments of his life, the significant and insignificant. He probably won't remember everything, but he'll remember you and the love he felt when you reached out to him with an accepting hug, or looked his way with a glowing glance, or gave him a proud pat on his head. He is your reward, and you are his.

A WORD FROM THE WORD:

Children are a gift from the Lord;
they are a reward from him.
PSALM 127:3 NLT

Think About It. . .

♥ Do you feel unappreciated? Most moms do occasionally—it's part of the job description: "Work more for less credit." If you sought job promotions, you'd never look in the Want Ads of Motherhood. Besides, any credit for your son's success goes to God. You work, but so does He. After all, He has two of you to raise: You and your son.

♥ Make the most of your moments. Like pennies in a fountain they may seem of little worth, but they amount to a whole lot of change over time.

♥ Your son will remember some incidents, but he'll remember his overall childhood experience from a general point of view. Create pleasing scenery.

FINAL THOUGHTS:

Author Dr. Kevin Leman wrote: "Childhood memories are one of the most reliable explanations of 'why you are the way you are.' These memories are like tapes playing in your head and they combine with the basic life-style you learned as a child to determine how you will respond to what happens to you every day."

Bless your boy with mounds of solid childhood memories. Of course, he'll have plenty of bad ones, too. That's part of living, grouped together with other imperfect people. But remember, he'll recall the whole and forget the bad parts—thank God!

• •

35. When in doubt, improvise.

• •

Raising a son is like walking blindfolded into unfamiliar territory. You never know what to expect. He will cajole you with his charm, amaze you with his intelligence, endear you with his love, humor you with his wit, unnerve you with his daring, and annoy you with his last-minute reminders.

At bedtime, your son suddenly remembers to tell you that he needs two dozen cookies the next day to take to school for a bake-sale fund-raiser. He had the note for weeks but *forgot* to give it to you. Or the coach calls and, with a calm but troubled voice, informs you that your son is hurt. His aggressive moves on the soccer field resulted in a broken ankle.

Your boy is a bundle of energy, aggressive in nature and unpredictable. He surprises you with his loving gestures and generosity, then exasperates you with his hyperactivity. So you find yourself starting to expect the unexpected.

With that, we learn to master the art of shortcuts. We concoct quick fixes in record time. As you whiz through the house, picking up stray socks, sorting piles of papers, and vacuuming cookie crumbs, your son whines: "Mommm, I'm hungry. When we gonna eat?" With only thirty minutes before you deliver him to soccer practice, try this quick recipe: Take everything from the left side of the fridge.

Combine all together. Put potato chips on top, and bake. Or, in a pinch, stopping for a McDonald's Happy Meal is just as good.

If your son needs a haircut, try a buzz cut. It needs no precision, just hair clippers with attachments. Or a bowl over the head works well for longer hair until he reaches about six years of age. That's when he will object, even if your pinking shears do a great job!

For his entertainment while you're in the car, empty Pringles cans serve as great containers for rolled-up paper and crayons, *and* they provide storage for smaller toys like Matchbox cars.

Learn to improvise. No one will care that the two dozen cookies you made for the school fundraiser were store bought. If his basketball uniform is unwashed, toss it in the dryer for a few minutes and, *voilà!* Sure, it may carry an odor, but it will anyway in short order.

At a moment's notice, smart moms know how to use what they have to serve their sons' needs. We devise games from household items. In a pinch, we create ways to occupy them. We don't worry about mishaps along the way; we expect them. It's all part of raising rambunctious boys. Moms, pat yourself on the back; we truly are the mothers of invention!

A WORD FROM THE WORD:

For we are God's masterpiece.
He has created us anew in Christ Jesus,
so we can do the good things he
planned for us along ago.
EPHESIANS 2:10 NLT

Think About It. . .

♡ The familiar axiom, "When life hands you a lemon, make lemonade," is applicable to moms of growing sons. No, sons aren't lemons (despite their sometimes sour dispositions), but they do conjure up some unsavory situations at times. If and when your son presents you with everything from a torn new pair of jeans to a gaping flesh wound the size of Texas, don't panic. Make lemonade and down it with a few Tylenols!

♡ God is your Creator. He created your son for His divine purposes. You, too, create ways to help, entertain, comfort, and care for your son in the midst of good and in the throes of bad circumstances and situations. Your creativity goes a long way. Use it.

♡ Does your son's impromptu nature cause havoc? Devise a list of do's and don'ts for him to follow. For instance: Do not wait until bedtime to give me school notes. Notes, papers, and announcements go from the book bag to a parent's hand immediately upon the child's entering the house from school.

FINAL THOUGHTS:

The unexpected isn't always a negative. In fact, some of the most brilliant inventions were discovered unexpectedly. Carl Sandburg noted: "Nearly all the best things that have come to me in life have been unexpected, unplanned by me." Some of the best times with your son will come from an unplanned event or an unexpected occurrence. A son presents challenges that are solved through improvisation, helping to stir a mom's latent creativity.

36. When stuff happens, don't panic. Well, maybe just a little.

Because boys tend to be reckless, hazards happen with frequency. But be assured, your son will probably survive, though it may not appear that way at the time.

Cassie recalls when her son stuck the rubber tip of an antenna into his tiny nose. The more she tried to remove it, the farther it lodged inside his nostril. Next stop, the emergency room. There the staff told Cassie and her husband to wait outside the hospital room while the pediatrician attempted to dislodge the rubber tip. Meanwhile Cassie, choking back tears, cringed with each scream her son bellowed. He made such a fuss, they had to wrap him in a straightjacket, which only intensified her anxiety. She broke down, sobbing while waiting outside the door, helpless to help him.

When Cassie's older son had emergency surgery at age nine for an ascended testicle, she thought she'd never make it through the night after the surgery. He cried in pain as she prayed aloud while trying to comfort her ailing boy—all night long. The following morning, her husband arrived and, as if on cue, it was smooth sailing. She returned home exhausted and emotionally drained, and her husband, refreshed and ready to go, sat by the hospital bed while her son suddenly fell peacefully asleep. Ugh!

Emergency room runs are normal for parents of boys. Jan's young son took a dive toward their family dog and hit his head on the corner of the coffee table. Blood gushed beneath the towel she pressed to his head as she and her husband drove him to the hospital. Lying on a gurney, her son whimpered as the doctor injected a shot into the open wound to numb it. Her husband, a robust manly man, stood at the foot of the bed and started to faint as he watched. The nurse, noticing the dad's queasiness, told him to go to the waiting room. "We don't need another patient," she said. He left while Jan stayed and watched the doctor stitch her little boy's head.

Boys run the gambit from scraped knees to minor concussions. Anything can and will happen as they test their daring. One boy tried to play Evel Knievel and jumped over a ramp with his dirt bike, an act which turned into a trip to the hospital for a slight concussion.

God has given moms an innate ability to rally when we have to, especially with boys. Although our first instinct is to panic, we find inner strength to gather our emotions and stay calm for our son's sake. Even if we're screaming inside, we usually don't show it.

The fact is, our sons will get through it, and so will we. It's all part of the growing process with boys. Remember they're audacious and often reckless. They test the limits, seldom realizing what the limits really are! We can warn them of the dangers, but we can't protect them from everything they might encounter or attempt.

Dr. James Dobson wrote, "One of the scariest aspects of raising boys is their tendency to risk life and limb for no good reason."

Boys are risk takers, rarely thinking before they engage in potentially dangerous actions. These are the boys who will, hopefully, grow into men who take risks for the kingdom of God. In the meantime, Mom, don't panic; he'll be just fine. Please God?

Think About It. . .

♡ Does your son seem to find danger effortlessly? Even though you childproof your home, your son isn't immune from life's mishaps. In fact, boys slip into them as easily as a hand to glove. Pray for him, do what you can to protect him, and entrust him to God's capable hands.

♡ Moms are made to think and act swiftly. They possess quick reflexes (they have to!). If you feel you aren't equipped to handle an emergency situation, think again. You are. God's grace is active the moment something happens, not before.

♡ Boys' assertive natures get them into trouble. Accept what you can't change, and change what you can.

FINAL THOUGHTS:

Boys seem to attract disaster. So it's frustrating when moms, who do so much to protect their sons, see them land on the rocky ground of life, bruised and bloody. But no need to panic. Most boys will make it through all the lumps and bumps of childhood. Just remember that you are not alone. When you dedicated your son to the Lord, promising to raise him according to the principles recorded in God's Word, God, too, promised to help and equip you for the job. And He does. Even when your son ends up in the ER.

37. Assure him that failure isn't an option; it's inevitable.

Winning matters to boys, big time. If your son fails to catch the ball at third base or he drops the football, he shoulders it and blames himself mercilessly. Boys are pressured to perform well, especially in sports or other masculine activities.

Your son wants to please you and your husband, even if he doesn't verbalize it. In fact, the more your son matures, the more he seeks his dad's approval. He knows he has yours. You are his best cheerleader. Yes, that's you cheering in the bleachers, even when your son fumbles the ball. But dads are more analytical and often live out their unfulfilled dreams through their sons. That places undue pressure on your boy.

Here's the reality: We have all failed and will fail again. It's a part of learning and growing. It's part of life. So here we stand with our boy who just failed at whatever was important to him. Jaw down to the ground, he beats himself up inside. There you are, Mom the encourager, trying to convince him that it's okay. Yet he's not buying it.

Your son views failure as a hit to his self-esteem. Ever watch the high-fives fly at a sports event when a group of boys score? Pumped with enthusiasm, they jump up and down, fists in the air. The moment they experience a failed attempt or missed opportunity, that same crew looks as if they were just dealt a death blow to the stomach.

So, Mom, among your other roles, you handle the situation as only you can. Teach him that failure is an opportunity for growth. Everyone fails at one time or another, even your son's dad. Help your boy to learn how to cushion the sting of failure. Instruct him that, contrary to the opinions of his peers and even some well-intentioned men in his life, winning *isn't* everything. To persevere in the face of defeat is more noteworthy. To keep trying when everything within him wants to quit, is more noble-minded. To maintain a positive, winning attitude is far more impressive than a three-point hoop! (Although his coach may feel otherwise, especially at a die-hard, must-win tournament game.)

Character, kindness, and good sportsmanship far outweigh the need to win, and losing is the catalyst that leads boys to become winners in the true sense of the word. Drive that home to your son. In doing so, you'll prepare him to become a genuine winner for Christ in the arena of life.

A WORD FROM THE WORD:

All athletes are disciplined in their training. They do it to win a prize that will fade away, but we do it for an eternal prize.
1 CORINTHIANS 9:25 NLT

Think About It. . .

💙 Encourage your son often. Underscore that all humans are prone to human failure. There is only one Person who will never fail: Jesus Christ. And He views your son as a winner in every way.

💙 If your son drowns himself in his own sorrow after a failed attempt, allow it for a limited amount of time. Give him space, then give him a talk. Peter, the rock on which Christ said He'd build His church, failed when he denied the Savior, his friend and Lord, three times. Can you imagine how he beat himself up over that? Yet afterward, he became a powerful force in the kingdom of God.

💙 Help your son learn from his mistakes and failures. Failure isn't the end; it's the start of a new beginning.

FINAL THOUGHTS:

No one likes to fail. Your son detests it. Yet failure is a stepping-stone to future success. John Keats wrote: "Don't be discouraged by a failure. It can be a positive experience. Failure is, in a sense, the highway to success, inasmuch as every discovery of what is false leads us to seek earnestly after what is true, and every fresh experience points out some form of error which we shall afterwards carefully avoid." Encourage your son to give it his best and not quit just because the going gets hard.

38. Prepare for it: Your idea of a vacation won't be your son's.

When you have young sons, your vacations, for the most part, are spent doing what the kids want to do. That's how it worked for my husband and me; however, I did insist that at least one day of our vacation time be spent touring something historical, hence educational. I didn't think that was too much to ask, but it was. My boys' argument against it was that they learned enough throughout the school year.

On one vacation, my two sons moaned, "Not another pioneer village." *Historical* translated into *hysterical* (and not in the funny sense) as smiles faded and energy levels plummeted.

"It's Lincoln's childhood home," I explained, which immediately initiated more whining.

"Do we *have* to go?"

"Do I *have* to watch you drive go-carts? Do I have to play arcade games with you? Do I have to jostle my innards on roller coasters and risk my life careening down water slides? Do I. . ."

"Okay, okay, Mom," they grumbled, "We'll go."

But they made me pay. Big time. Our day of tourism consisted of four hours of one-way family interaction. The kids sighed deeply and walked as fast as garden slugs, shuffling their feet behind me.

"Hey, look," I announced with exuberance as I scanned the brochure. "It says here that this is the log building where Lincoln first practiced law."

No one responded, not even my husband. As we strolled through another exhibit, I turned to my husband to relay a morsel of historical trivia. "Uh-huh," he grumbled, forcing a grin. Soon after I overheard father and sons commiserating. Husband Jim consoled the kids, whispering things like, "I know, I know. It won't be long now. Mom's almost done and we'll go to the pool when we get back to the hotel."

You'd think I sentenced them to forced labor. Over lunch, I tucked the pamphlet beside my plate to chart our next destination.

"I'm hot," son Jeff whimpered.

"We're in air-conditioning," I said through clenched teeth.

"So how much more is left to see?" hubby asked not so discreetly.

With that, I stuck the brochure inside my purse and announced that we would leave right after lunch. Suddenly, chatter and peals of laughter filled the table. The temperature was perfect, the setting divine, and I was no longer vacationing alone.

Visiting historical places or doing something educational was as appealing to my boys as eating raw broccoli. After another vacation war, wisdom told me to prepare for vacations and discuss our plans *beforehand.* Then we'd make the experience fun, incorporating activities for everyone to enjoy—only if the boys refrained from complaining. If they violated that rule, some other activity the boys relished might disappear from the vacation to-do list!

A WORD FROM THE WORD:

For I am afraid that when I come I won't like what I find, and you won't like my response. I am afraid that I will find quarreling, jealousy, anger, selfishness. . .and disorderly behavior.
2 CORINTHIANS 12:20 NLT

Think About It. . .

♡ Did you ever dread a family vacation? Kids are selfish, but they're also kids. Give them instructions, but brace yourself for some of their temporary bouts of self-absorption.

♡ Vacations should be fun, but too often they become battlefields of too much activity, tired, whiney kids, and petty arguments. To ward off wars, plan ahead. Pack plenty of downtime activities for the boys and take that time to rest yourself.

♡ Tell your boys what's expected. If they whine while doing something you enjoy, tell them that you will limit or remove an activity they want to do. Remind them that this is your vacation, too.

FINAL THOUGHTS:

Truth is, even as believers, moms can become selfish, too. Have you ever stomped your spiritual foot and said, "But God, I don't want to do that!" when you sensed a nudge from the Holy Spirit to do something you'd rather not do? Everyone complains and grumbles from time to time, and growing sons are no different. In fact, they're great at it. Before a trip, sit down as a family and agree on what you'll do and where you'll go. Underscore the importance of doing activities that will interest everyone, not just them.

• •

39. Don't underestimate your role.

• •

You might think that to properly raise a son, one needs an involved dad. Ideally, that's true. But we live in an imperfect world occupied by imperfect people. Images straight out of a Norman Rockwell painting are quaint and beautiful, but they are just that—images.

Mom, your role in your son's life is influential to his growth, maturity, and overall well-being. Way back in 1865, William Wallace wrote: "The hand that rocks the cradle rules the world." The often-quoted poem praised moms for the lasting and constant power they had to mold and shape their children's lives.

Okay, I admit that it doesn't often feel that way. Yep, at times it feels as if the one who rules your world is your rambunctious son. You may rock the cradle, but he is far from slumber and submission. Your first clue comes every morning when you drag out of bed and he leaps up with the energy of a squirrel gathering nuts. You make him breakfast that he doesn't want to eat, pack his school lunch that you are certain he doesn't eat, and make sure he is dressed in something other than his pajama bottoms and a T-shirt before driving him to school. After school you chauffeur him from one point to another, like connecting dots on a map. In between and all the while, you teach, instruct, remind, repeat yourself, pray, repeat yourself, extinguish sibling arguments, and subdue out-of-control roughhousing.

Regardless, our objective is to raise our sons not only to physical maturity (that happens all by itself) but emotional and spiritual manhood. And as unimaginable and impossible it might seem, that's exactly what you're doing. I know, it's hard to imagine that your fist-bumping, high-fiving, video-playing, rowdy, reckless boy will grow to become a responsible, well-adjusted man, but he will with your help and God's amazing grace.

You play an integral role in your son becoming a godly, successful, honorable man. Your instruction, discipline, and love serve as a trusted guide and constant companion. Don't minimize it, even when you're scraping off chunks of clay from the bottom of his soccer shoes. Your efforts may just produce a man capable of ruling the world one day.

A WORD FROM THE WORD:

Listen, my son, to your father's instruction
and do not forsake your mother's teaching.
PROVERBS 1:8 NIV

Think About It. . .

♡ Moms carry the weight and the worry of raising kids. Frustration and anger surface during times of stress or when moms overextend ourselves (which is just about daily). You won't ruin your son with your occasional outbursts. He's tougher than you think. When things calm down, discuss your feelings, issue apologies (if warranted), and move on.

♡ Can you think of ways to contribute to your son's spiritual and emotional growth? For instance: Consider sharing a short devotional before school (during breakfast); remember to hug and encourage him daily; select one of his best attributes and discuss how you can help him use his gift to help others.

♡ Your son looks to you more than you realize. Be there for him; he needs you.

FINAL THOUGHTS:

Most moms don't realize the impact they have on their son's life. He's watching his dad or other father figures, not you, right? Wrong. You are instrumental in his spiritual and emotional growth, his sense of security, belonging, love, and acceptance.

Did you ever listen to what a football star, celebrity, or world-class athlete has to say after winning an award or recognition? Typically, he acknowledges and thanks his mother first and foremost. Your son feels your influence every day and will continue to do so throughout his life. You are making an impact in unseen but powerful ways.

• •

40. Instill solid work ethics.

• •

"Ah," you say, "this tip is for his dad." You're right. Dads are living, breathing, outstanding examples to their sons in many categories of son-rearing. Boys look to their dads at an early age, emulating their speech, mannerisms, and actions. But teaching your son solid work ethics is your privilege and responsibility, too.

You might not be able to show him how to change the oil in your car or how to use a power tool (then again, maybe you are one of those industrious ladies who can!). But you can teach him the importance of hard work. After all, you want to prepare him for a lifetime of work to support his family not only at the workplace, but in his home.

In fact, did you ever notice communication between two men who just met each other? "What's your line of work?" is one of the first questions they ask. A man's career or job defines him; it promotes and enhances self-esteem.

If you haven't done so already, assign chores. (See Tip 25.) Start as early as possible. But brace yourself, because he'll probably make more of a mess than be of help. And that's okay. Just grin, grit your teeth, and let him do the best he can. He's learning to work. Delegate responsibilities you know he can fulfill, like picking up his toys, making his bed, taking out the garbage, cleaning off the dinner table, raking leaves, or even painting something. Warning: If you allow the painting, use drop cloths generously.

If your son helps out around the house in which he's been raised, he's more apt to continue that after he's grown and married. It also garners a sense of responsibility and of a job well done. On the other hand, the mom who waits on her son hand-and-foot produces a guy who will expect his wife to do the same.

If that doesn't move you to consider your son's work ethics, try this: Imagine your son twenty years from now, ordering his wife to "Get me another soda [or worse, a beer] with my sausage sandwich, will ya?" In that scenario, his wife will blame you, and rightly so.

Reward his work with incentives. When he's old enough, give him an allowance or treat him with a trip to his favorite restaurant or ice-cream place. This will show him that you appreciate his efforts and that hard work pays off.

Teaching your son the value of work engages him and gives him a sense of responsibility, well-being, and belonging. So begin early and continue until he leaves home.

A WORD FROM THE WORD:

Whatever your hand finds to do,
do it with all your might.
ECCLESIASTES 9:10 NIV

Think About It. . .

♥ One mom quoted the above verse so much to her sons that they would mouth the phrase as soon as she verbalized the first two words. Although your son may tire of your constant insistence to perform a task or duty, he will respond to your consistent instructions when you give him praise and positive reinforcement.

♡ Do you give your son age-appropriate duties? Even a small child can pick up his toys or help feed the cat. Increase his chores as he ages. Create a list for him, and discuss the importance of contributing to the household. Encourage him to dust, take care of the dog, wash the car, or clean windows.

♡ Show your son the value of hard work. Don't give him everything he wants; make him earn it. Does he want a new bike or an iPod? Offer age-appropriate jobs he can do to make some cash. Does an elderly neighbor need yard work done? How about shoveling sidewalks and driveways? Present ideas to awaken the latent entrepreneur in him.

FINAL THOUGHTS:

According to scriptures, laziness is a sin. Instilling a strong work ethic in your son blesses him and others in the long run. Hardworking dads emulate strong work ethics, but so do hard-working moms. Of course, there are no guarantees. You can assign your son chores, encourage him to get a part-time job in his teenager years, and do everything right. But the choice to work and how much he'll devote to his job is up to him after he's on his own. At the very least, it's up to moms to give our sons a hearty jump start.

41. Invite him to join you in the kitchen.

In this day and age, we understand that the kitchen isn't exclusive to women. Of course we still gravitate toward teaching our daughters kitchen basics, but sons need a few lessons of their own, too.

The fascination with stirring, pouring, and making messes is fun for your son. Granted, the stirring, pouring, and messes are often dirt related: Shoveling dirt into any conceivable container then pouring it out everywhere is visceral boy behavior. But for a moment, remember how your little boy loved to stir up imaginary recipes during bath-time play?

Little "Chef Boy Ian," the name he gave himself, had his grandmother record his homemade bath recipe as follows: "Cucumbers, two squashes, two light blue dolphins, one blue whale, one purple octopus, and one pink fish. Put the yellow soap in the red bowl until it is all foggy. Add one hundred scoops of water, then one more scoop of water, mix it up, and put it in the oven for one minute and seventeen seconds. That's all of my ingredients!" Yes, give your young son an old Tupperware bowl and plastic spoon in the bathtub and watch him create bubble-bath soup.

Your son is at the age where he actually wants to help. Encourage kitchen duties. Begin with the basics. Allow him to stir, pour, and measure at first. Then advance toward teaching him how to use cutlery safely and allow him to chop something easy to cut up. Warning: Keep an observant eye open, because things could get out of hand, so to speak.

Cooking is an important skill for your son to learn. Teaching him how to prepare a meal helps him on his road to independence. By the time he becomes a teenager, he should be able to cook a few meals himself, even though he'll leave your stainless steel appliances and once-spotless countertops laden with grease splatters, smudges, and food particles everywhere.

Meanwhile, make cooking fun. Preschool and elementary-age boys are creative. Let your son accompany you grocery shopping. Give him a list and let him help you find items. Later, combine the ingredients you bought and cook or bake something together. Male chef and nutritionist Jamie Oliver created a Nintendo DS cooking game for boys. The video instructs boys how to make different recipes and allows the player to build a shopping list for the recipe he'd like to try.

Cooking together is a family activity that initiates conversation and demonstrates love. Fond, heartwarming memories are simmered in the relaxing atmosphere of a kitchen filled with laughter, chatter, and the smell of delicious works in progress.

The point is that the kitchen isn't exclusive to females. Some of the best chefs are men. At a young age, your son can manage easy tasks like stirring batter, setting the table, and helping to wash dishes. He can even learn to make his own peanut butter and jelly sandwich. As he gets older, teach him how to prepare simple stovetop meals. Familiarize him with kitchen duties and watch him take charge. You might just lose your role as chief chef and bottle washer!

A WORD FROM THE WORD:

Better a small serving of vegetables
with love than a fattened calf with hatred.
PROVERBS 15:17 NIV

Think About It. . .

♡ Ask your son what he'd like to make. Search a kids' cookbook for easy, fun recipes.

♡ Does your son show an interest for cooking? Take advantage of it before his curiosity turns to other things.

♡ After you let him do fun things like sifting flour or rolling out small lumps of pastry dough, praise him for his efforts.

FINAL THOUGHTS:

It takes time and patience to teach your son how to cook, but the time you invest now will pay dividends later. One mom said that in her family of two boys and one girl, her sons learned how to cook, while her daughter never showed any interest until she married. Throughout their childhoods, the two sons emulated the joys of cooking and later, much to their wives' delight, became chief chefs in their own households.

42. Attack the issue, not the individual.

The pressures of mothering sons, or children in general, are beyond taxing. So it stands to reason that our nerves sometimes unravel easier than a spool of yarn.

For instance: You've spent all day cleaning the house, grocery shopping, and running errands on your day off work. You're exhausted and would love nothing more than to sit quietly for a few minutes alone. But it's time to pick up your son from school. As soon as he walks through the backdoor, he tosses his book bag, duffle tote, and coat in a heap. Before you can instruct him to pick up his mess, he's chomping on potato chips as he heads for his room, leaving a crumb trail behind. You meet him at his doorway and issue instructions to take care of his mess. "Besides," you remind him, "since when do we dart for the junk food as soon as we get home?"

He assures you he'll clean up while you start dinner. You have an evening appointment and still need to shower and get ready. With dinner on the stove, you nudge your son, who still lingers in his bedroom, to start his homework and, by the way, pick up his mess? Time is ticking and your heart rate accelerates with so much to do before you have to leave. Your son nonchalantly exits his room, still downing a bag of chips. You begin to seethe as fatigue, frustration, and the day itself closes in on you.

Now you are in explosion mode. Anything will set you off, and it does. Built-up emotions from the day, or possibly week, arise to the surface in hot pursuit, and your son is the target.

It's seldom one thing that causes us to vent in anger or frustration. Moms deal with a lot. The problem is, when we unleash upon our son, we're attacking him instead of the issues.

In this case, the concern is disobedience. You asked him three things: to pick up his mess, stop eating junk before dinner, and start his homework. Because you were so busy with other things—and he knew it—he failed to comply.

It's difficult but wise for us to attack the *issues*, not the individual. When we attack our son, we usually find ourselves spewing unkind, derogatory comments in a fit of anger. But when we attack the issue—in this case disobedience—we hold him accountable for his behavior instead.

What issues irritate you? Your son's forgetfulness? His unkempt bedroom? Poor grades when you know he has the capacity to do much better? Laziness? Outright defiance or disobedience?

Regardless, if you attack the issues rather than your son, you will help him learn to change bad habits. But when you attack him you risk damaging his spirit. Too many of those repeated onslaughts produce lots of other issues down the line. And who needs more issues with which to deal? Every mom has enough already.

A WORD FROM THE WORD:

And who can win this battle against the world?
Only those who believe that Jesus is the Son of God.
1 JOHN 5:5 NLT

Think About It. . .

♡ Moms are in spiritual battle. Pray for your son. He has issues and so do you. Don't allow your issues to become a battering ram against your son the moment he does something wrong. Take your issues, and his, to God in prayer. After all, the Lord can deal with anything. Your threshold for problems is limited.

♡ What issues set you off? Establish rules and guidelines for your son to follow. Then consistently administer godly discipline when he breaks them. If you allow your emotions to fester and build, you're sure to explode eventually. Avoid arriving at the point of no return.

♡ Deal with the issue immediately. If you wait, things will fester. Address his disobedience before one act of defiance or pure forgetfulness turns into several.

FINAL THOUGHTS:

Daily pressures and stresses are part of everyday life. Your growing son is just being himself. Most of the time, he doesn't even realize he is doing something to push you off the edge. Address the issues. It takes practice, especially in the heat of the moment; so rather than bombarding your boy when he misbehaves or disobeys, deal with each problem immediately. The late Peter Marshall prayed, "When we long for life without difficulties, remind us that oaks grow strong in contrary winds and diamonds are made under pressure." Face it: A few years of motherhood turns every woman into a strong oak dripping with diamonds!

• •

43. If he takes something apart, hand him a tool.

• •

Did you ever watch your son play with blocks? He stacks them only to knock them down seconds later. He loves to build, but the thrill comes with the destruction of his creation. A sand castle lasts for a few minutes before he smashes it into a pile.

Boys also love to take things apart. Steve Jobs said, "Older people sit down and ask, 'What is it?' but the boy asks, 'What can I do with it?'" Give your son a bike and he inspects the wheels, spokes, and chains. Hand him a toy and he looks for ways to dismantle it.

Although your son wants to know what he can do with a toy or object, mostly he wants to know what makes it work. His curiosity comes to play whenever he plays. To the chagrin of many moms, their school-age sons' inquisitiveness may result in the destruction of home electronic devices or even the basic flashlight. Although disassembling objects isn't necessarily an accurate indication of his future career choice, you wonder if your current little Tim-the-Tool-Man might just, in later years, become the next Surgeon General.

Yes, boys seem to have an innate desire to dissect things. They probe to see how a clock works. If your son shows such an interest, allow him to join Dad in the garage to help change the oil or whatever else men do out there! It's great experience for your son and a bonding time with his dad.

Should you have something to assemble, solicit your son's help.

Hand him a screwdriver (if he's old enough), and show him how to use it. After your project is complete, stand back and observe as your son beams with pride and a sense of accomplishment. In fact, he'll likely ask if you have any more items to screw together or take apart. Count on it.

At a funeral, one elementary-age boy approached his great-grandfather's casket and began to lift the lining. Immediately, his dad came from behind and chided him. "But I just wanted to see what was underneath," the boy explained. He didn't mean to act disrespectful or inappropriate. His curiosity just got the best of him.

Your son wants to know how things work. Tell him. Better yet, hand him a tool and allow him to find out.

A WORD FROM THE WORD:

The Lord your God has blessed you
in all of the work of your hands.
DEUTERONOMY 2:7 NIV

Think About It. . .

♡ Curiosity is a noble attribute when used correctly and channeled in a positive direction. Although "curiosity killed the cat" and misdirection could do major damage, encourage your son's curiosity and manage his use of it.

♡ Is your son fascinated with everything from dissecting frogs to analyzing ants? Does he love to dismantle things? With proper guidance, you can use his fascination to teach him. Who knows? Someday his curiosity might lead him to find the cure for cancer.

♡ Select toys that encourage him in his building pursuits. Toy tools, Lego sets (offer everything from pirate to Star War ships), Erector sets, blocks, and models are great for up-and-coming little construction workers.

FINAL THOUGHTS:

Your son is curious. That means he has an innate desire to explore, dissect, examine, research, and study. He's not satisfied with watching, he requires hands-on involvement. Help him in his pursuits. It's a good thing that's good for him.

44. Read to him early and often.

From the time James was seven months old, his grandmother and mom read to him. Lying on the floor, his grandmother held him in the crux of her arm with an open book. Amazingly, he'd lie peacefully, gazing wide-eyed at the illustrated pictures. While his parents worked, the grandmother spent hours caring for, playing with, and reading to her grandson.

At the age of four, James began to read everything, from newspaper headlines to storefront and billboard signs. Knowing he'd read anything within his sightline, while they drove down the highway, his parents tried to avert him from seeing questionable signs.

As James grew older, he continued to read. Even as a teen he was rarely seen without a book in hand. He loved fictional series and science books. And he collected books like some kids collect video games. While he gravitated toward Xbox games like most of the boys his age, he still loved the joy of reading.

So how do you get your son to read, especially when he's spiked into overdrive? Begin reading to him early and do so daily. Bedtime stories, Bible stories, and all the stories in between will encourage a love of books. Select ones with topics of interest to him, such as dinosaurs, horses, planes, cars, sports, or trucks. Boys love adventure stories with fast-paced plots and characters. Nonfiction action stories, suspense, and science fiction attract them as well. Remember that he's more apt to read something that ignites his curiosity and piques his interest.

Boys find it hard to sit for long periods of time. They're geared to run, jump, swing, and bounce (usually off the walls and such).

Reading helps to slow him down. It also brings much-needed peace and quiet to you and calmness to him.

Make reading fun and interesting. Engage him through play acting; become the story's characters using different voices for each one. Make books a part of his daily life. Are you a reader? If so, him watching you read will increase his desire to do the same.

And don't forget the most important reading of all: the Bible. Daily Bible reading will introduce him to God's Word and show him the importance of learning scriptural principles and memorizing Bible verses. Christian bookstores and websites are loaded with age-appropriate Bibles and books. So read often and begin early!

A WORD FROM THE WORD:

"Study this Book of Instruction continually. Meditate on it day and night so you will be sure to obey everything written in it. Only then will you prosper and succeed in all you do."
JOSHUA 1:8 NLT

Think About It. . .

♡ Search garage sales and flea markets for used books. Buy in bulk. The more selections you have, the more choices he has. What may not interest him today might captivate him six months later.

♡ Make frequent trips to the library or bookstore. Bookstores have children's sections designed to intrigue your child. Many offer a story hour with group readings or programs created to enhance your son's reading experience.

♡ Make sure his reading material is within his range of comprehension, interest, and ability. If it's too hard to read, he won't.

FINAL THOUGHTS:

Reading should be fun and enjoyable. All too often it's just the opposite, especially for boys who'd rather climb hills than peruse books. Well-rounded kids need both activities. After all, long after he ceases to climb hills, books will still teach and entertain him.

● ●

45. Who's the boss?
Remember that you are.

● ●

Why is it that some boys run roughshod over their moms while others practically stand to attention with one discerning look from their moms? It's simple. The former mom allows her son to rule the roost, while the latter reigns over the entire hen house—her little rooster included.

A pecking order exists in every area of our lives: From the homeroom to the boardroom, someone is in charge. God's pecking order goes something like this: God first; others second—namely our husband, then our children. The Lord gives us parental authority over our children, not to dominate and control them, but to guide, instruct, teach, discipline, and love them. He entrusts them to our care for a short period of time, to raise them to know Him and follow His principles to become men of integrity.

Count on it: Your son will test your will, your patience, and challenge your authority. Not just one time, but many! Without your loving discipline and direction, he'll defy you and other authority figures throughout his lifetime should his actions go without consequences now.

Dr. James Dobson stated: "By learning to yield to the loving authority of his parents, a child learns to submit to other forms of authority which will confront him later in his life—his teachers, school principal, police, neighbors and employers."

From the time my two boys were small, they understood who was boss. Oh sure, they tested my husband and me repeatedly, but we held fast to our authority, like a trained soldier guarding the camp. We gave them freedom with boundaries, but when they started to cross the line we held firm.

Often my sons took liberties to misbehave and test their limits, especially in public places where they thought they could get away with it. But I was an expert at leveling "the look." You know, that glare, stare, or expression that fosters obedience faster than a scared rabbit. The look speaks louder than words. It says, "Don't even think of it!" or "Stop it. Now!" My sons recognized the look and knew exactly what to do. Administering it at just the right moment produced instantaneous results.

Boys need to know who is boss. Author and speaker Jerry Jenkins overheard his son speaking to his toy action figure: "If you die in this mission," the boy said, "you can ask Jesus for anything you want, and if it's all right with your mom, He'll give it to you!" Wow! This young boy knew who ruled their roost!

Regardless of your son's age, don't tolerate bad behavior. If you do, you open the door to years of battling his smart-aleck attitude and rebellious ways. Lovingly teach him respect for authority now. As you teach him to respect your authority, he will respect God's authority and learn to submit to all future authority figures in his life. And above all, level "the look" as needed.

A WORD FROM THE WORD:

He must manage his own family well,
having children who respect and obey him.
1 TIMOTHY 3:4 NLT

Think About It. . .

♡ Ask yourself: Who's the boss in my home? Does my son run rampant? Do I implement and enforce house rules?

♡ God is the final supreme authority. As you submit to Him, you learn to mother your son more effectively. Are you having trouble keeping your son under submission? Begin today to make needed changes in your submission to God and your son's to you.

♡ Discuss with your husband how to better handle your son.

Involved dads are instrumental in their boys' lives. If one with God is a majority, consider what the two of you can accomplish with God's help!

FINAL THOUGHTS:

Each person is born with a sinful nature. Disobedience and defiance comes naturally to your son. If you allow him to, he'll trample you underfoot like packed snow. Your job is to set standards and rules for him to follow, and lovingly implement them. That's not to say that you should run a dictatorship household. A good leader instructs, teaches, and uses his or her authority to help, not hurt. A godly mother runs her household with love. Exercising and maintaining your authority in the home helps your son learn submission to all authority.

• •

46. Accept it: Lizards, snakes, and geckos fascinate boys. Oh my!

• •

Eight-year-old Trevor's family vacationed in Hawaii where Trevor's uncle lived. Geckos, a common lizard on Maui, make themselves right at home indoors. While Trevor was sitting in his uncle's living room one day, a distinct clicking sound echoed from the kitchen. Trevor jumped to see what it was while his wide-eyed mom inquired, "What's that?"

"Oh, that's a gecko," the uncle said in a matter-of-fact manner.

"In the house?"

"Don't worry," he assured her. "They don't hurt anything."

The locals allow the intrusive reptile into their homes and have done so for generations. According to legend, geckos are a sign of good luck. Although Trevor's uncle denounced the tradition, he allowed the critter to inhabit his home without rebuff. "Geckos are to us what ladybugs are to you," he explained. "You wouldn't think to kill a ladybug, would you?"

"Frankly, yes," the mom replied, unconvinced.

Meanwhile, Trevor was in reptile heaven. Analyzing the slithery green creature, his compassion was evident. "Come on, Mom, just look at him, he won't hurt you," he repeated, his eyes transfixed on his new little friend.

The rest of the trip consisted of bouts of begging. "Please, Mom, can we take him home? Can I have a gecko in our house?"

Reptiles and amphibians attract boys. Anything slithery and slimy that jumps or crawls fascinates them. While the sight of crawling things may repulse some of us women, causing us to run to the hills, screaming in trepidation, our son will stoop down for closer examination. And actually handling the slithery creature is more fascinating and exciting to him than his launching from the top of a bunk bed onto the floor.

Even as boys turn to young men, the fascination continues. Some guys tattoo images of snakes crawling up their arm. Retailers even sell sheets and blankets with snakes and lizards on them. Can you imagine a little girl purchasing those items to adorn her pink room with ruffled curtains? Nope. Reptiles are boy magnets.

And so it is, Mom. As Trevor's mom and uncle continued to discuss the clicking creature, she asked her brother what would happen if Trevor's gecko friend decided to invite relatives. "Oh, yeah," her brother responded undisturbed, "there's already another one in here somewhere."

Mom checked the floor and ceiling around her. "Get rid of those geckos!" she blurted out in fear. "Shoo them out of here!"

Trevor's uncle shook his head and grinned a you're-making-something-out-of-nothing smile. Meanwhile, Trevor embarked on a search-and-find for any possible "family members."

A WORD FROM THE WORD:

Lizards—they are easy to catch,
but they are found even in kings' palaces.
PROVERBS 30:28 NLT

Think About It. . .

♡ Pet gerbils are one thing; pet lizards and snakes are quite another, at least for most moms. Yet your little guy might derive a lot of pleasure caring for one of those creatures. No big deal if you can accept the idea and the reptile is harmless and handled properly. Just make sure he understands that he, not you, is responsible for his pet of preference.

♡ Does your son beg you for a pet frog, snake, or lizard but you can't bring yourself to buy one? Frequent a pet shop that keeps these creatures and let him engage in some friendly interaction. Tell him that you will "visit" often.

FINAL THOUGHTS:

Wasn't it a snake that tempted Eve in the garden and got humankind into this sinful mess? And here you are in a battle of the wills with your son whose one desire is to own a slithering, creepy crawler. The attraction is difficult for most moms to understand, let alone allow. Just remember that this is just another phase. Soon he'll be fascinated with girls instead. Hmm, maybe you should rethink the reptile issue.

• •

47. Attend church regularly, even when it's a hassle.

• •

The kids are yelling, the dog is barking, and breakfast is burning while you scurry to get yourself and your kids ready for church. What a hassle! You're tempted to throw your hands up, wave the white apron strings of surrender, and just stay home, sit back, and pour a second cup of java. It sure would be a lot easier.

Once you arrive at church, though, you're glad you braved the family elements, which can be much worse than rain, sleet, or snow.

The church service was just the boost you needed, and to know your son benefited from children's church while you were immersed in fellowship and worship made all the home-front havoc worthwhile.

And so the question: Do you have to attend church to call yourself a Christian? Nope. If you've asked God for forgiveness and accepted Christ into your heart, you are God's own. At the same time, gathering together with other like-minded believers enhances your spiritual growth and provides the fellowship you need. And if you need that, how much more does your son?

Regular church attendance helps bolster your son's faith. It reinforces the biblical principles you teach him at home. Church helps him connect and interact with kids his age as they hear God's Word, worship the Lord, and pray together. In God's House he has the opportunity for involvement in church-related activities.

Someone asked the son of a preacher if he ever tired of attending all those services while growing up. His response? "Church attendance was all I knew. When it was Sunday or Wednesday evening, we were there. I never gave any thought to *not* going."

Attending church is like anything else you do routinely. It's Sunday, and you pack up the family and go to church. Sometimes the car ride on the way gets hairy as siblings banter back and forth, and nerves fray as you rush to arrive on time. But it all pays off.

Although church attendance can't take the place of living your faith daily before your son, it teaches him the importance of his family interacting with the family of God and participating in the act of worship. So attend Sunday. Pack up the family and make church a priority—you'll be glad you did.

A WORD FROM THE WORD:

And let us not neglect our meeting together, as some people do, but encourage one another, especially now that the day of his return is drawing near.
HEBREWS 10:25 NLT

- ♡ If you are unaccustomed to regular church attendance, your son may resist going at first. Commit to going together weekly or twice weekly. Soon, church attendance will become as natural as brushing his teeth or, more likely, as natural as eating his favorite dessert.

- ♡ If you haven't already, find a church that offers plenty of kid-related activities and Sunday school classes. What blesses you will probably bore your son. But age-appropriate classes or children's church make learning the Bible fun.

FINAL THOUGHTS:

You teach your son about the Lord through your example. The most important element of his spiritual growth is a mom and dad who love each other and love God. Can you love God and not attend church? Yes. But giving him the foundation of becoming involved with a church family and all that entails instills the importance of worshipping God, serving Him, and fellowshipping with other believers.

- -

48. When your son gets sick, treat him special (if you dare).

- -

What's worse than watching your son suffer with a cold, the stomach flu, or (the unthinkable) surgery? Our maternal instincts kick into overdrive when our little guys are ill. If we could, we'd transfer their awful symptoms to ourselves in a blink of a watery eye.

Years ago when one of my then small boys got sick, I'd make a bed for him on the couch. Snuggled beneath layers of blankets, he had everything he needed: a glass of fruit juice, a box of tissues, the thermometer, the television remote, and "the bell."

The bell was my biggest mistake. Initially, I thought it would help the infirmed and me. Its availability to my sick son meant I could easily perform household chores in the remotest areas of our home and still hear him if he needed me. Yep, that's what I thought and here's what happened.

I'd serve chicken soup and saltines, fill his juice glass, take his temperature, dispense the medicine, fluff the pillow, and ask, "Is there anything else you need, sweetie?"

Eyes transfixed on the television, my sick child would slurp down the soup and shake his head "no." Confident all was well, I'd get to work for about five minutes until. . .*ring-a-ling-ling, ring-a-ling-ling*.

"What's wrong?" I'd ask, having dropped everything to run couch-side.

"Can I have some Jell-O?" he'd say, handing me the empty soup bowl.

After dishing up the dessert, I'd tuck the blanket under his chin and ask the anything-else question again. Great, back to work. Minutes later. . .*the bell.*

"What is it!?" I'd yell through the house, becoming increasingly impatient.

In the distance I'd hear a whiny, nasal voice.

"What did you say?" I'd ask, walking closer.

"I saaaaaid, I can't find the remote control," he'd whimper with a look of abandonment. Without fail, the strain of having to raise his voice weakened his body as he struggled to position himself with feeble movements. Amazingly, one tiny porcelain bell turned an otherwise dutiful child into an ornery, self-centered brat.

About this time, my compassion for him turned the corner and headed for the door. The bell I gave him morphed into a weapon aimed at destroying my tolerance and needling my nerves.

After repeatedly misusing the bell, my son finally got the message when I refused to answer. Eventually, I confiscated the ring-a-ling altogether.

Boys enjoy being waited on. So do husbands. Let's face it, we all do. We instinctively desire to take care of our ailing sons within reason. But when you nurse your son, remember, even the most docile child can, and will, turn into a tyrant if you allow him. I regretted handing my son the bell and didn't do it again. Even when he asked for it, which happens once you open the door to self-imposed slavery.

Some of us pray with a bell mentality. Whenever we ask the Lord for something, we expect immediate results and instant answers. Make no mistake, God listens, but He doesn't always answer the way we'd expect or like. Nevertheless, our bell mentality remains because, unlike a pushed-to-her-limit mom, God is long-suffering. Achew! I mean, amen to that.

A WORD FROM THE WORD:

And even when you ask, you don't get it because your motives are all wrong—you want only what will give you pleasure.
JAMES 4:3 NLT

Think About It. . .

♡ Boys are especially whiney when they're ill. That's normal and expected. Dote on him if you dare.

♡ When your son is sick, he'll require more of your time and ultimately test your patience (especially as he gets better and still acts sick). Give him the kind of attention he needs. Rock him, even if you don't do that normally (unless, of course, he's bigger than you). He needs his mom's soothing words and gentle manner.

♡ Good health comes with proper hygiene. Teach your son to wash his hands or use hand sanitizer at school before he eats and after he uses the restroom. Of course, if he'd use it more often than that, great! But don't hold your breath.

FINAL THOUGHTS:

It's a fact of life: No matter what you do to prevent it, sickness happens. Your kids catch the flu with the ease of a sneeze and the grace of a raging bull. Dona Maddux Cooper reminds one of how fleeting the days are when one has the opportunity to protect and care for a son: "When you were small and just a touch away, I covered you with blankets against the cold night air. But now that you are tall and out of reach, I fold my hands and cover you with prayer." So go ahead and treat him special; he needs it. Just refrain from giving him a ringing instrument.

- -

49. Spend time with your son; it's never wasted.

- -

The childhood memory was transfixed in his mind. James Boswell, the famous biographer of Samuel Johnson, often spoke of the boyhood day his father took him fishing. He remembered the pristine delight of sitting with his dad alongside a lazy creek bed. Together, they whittled away time as carefree as a wood carver shaves a piece of discarded kindling.

Boswell recounted his experience repeatedly throughout his life, reflecting on the storehouse of knowledge his dad imparted to him that day as they eyed their cork bobbers in anticipation of a tug on their fishing lines.

Hearing Boswell's fishing experience so frequently, a friend thought to check the daily journal that Boswell's father kept to ascertain—from a parent's perspective—what the dad said about the father-son excursion. Turning to the date, the inquirer found one sentence: "Gone fishing today with my son; a day wasted."

As you sit at the park and watch your son repeatedly climb the stairs to the slide, or push him on the swing and he shouts, "Higher, Mom!" do you ever glance at your watch, feeling as if this tedious activity is a waste of precious time? Instead of playing catch with him, you could be weeding the garden; rather than constructing Legos, you could work on your household budget and pay bills.

Every mom, every parent, has felt time frittering away while accompanying their son in mindless activities. With all the daily responsibilities today's mom shoulders, it's tough to step on the breaks long enough to dabble in child's play. "What a frivolous waste of time and energy," we mutter as we begrudgingly succumb to our son's pleas to enter the world of make-believe. In his world, clocks and adult responsibilities are as extinct as the dinosaurs with which he plays.

Yet the activities you might view as futile produce lasting memories for your son. And face it, don't we all need a little more make-believe injected into our stressful lives?

The most insignificant mother-son interactions last a lifetime: catching lightning bugs in a jar, bicycling to Dairy Queen, lighting sparklers on the Fourth of July, praying together before the big game.

What means little to us, counts to them. And the only thing that is worse than a mom's false perception of wasted time is regrets.

A WORD FROM THE WORD:

He has made everything beautiful in its time.
ECCLESIASTES 3:11 NIV

Think About It. . .

♡ One of the best gifts you can give your children is your time. Worldly wisdom celebrates quality time over quantity. God's wisdom extols both quality and quantity. Just knowing you are in the next room gives your child a sense of well-being and security.

♡ Is there something you do with your child that you feel is a waste of time? Be honest. Jot those things down on paper and take a closer look. Develop a new perspective.

♡ Do you play silly games with your son while driving down the street? When are the times that initiate the most conversations? Those are the moments you might overlook or underestimate but your son will remember and cherish.

FINAL THOUGHTS:

Time is at a minimum. With all the technology to make your life more convenient, easier, and faster, you've slipped into a continuum of too much to do and not enough time to do it. You live in a face-paced society. Slow down and redirect how you spend your time.

50. Beware: Your son's toy of choice might come back to taunt and haunt.

Boys gravitate to toys with noise. And if the sound of the toy is too soft, your son will manufacture louder versions. Assemble a cardboard airplane and he will make roaring noises so loud, you'll think a 747 landed on your street. Riding toys come complete with *clickety-clack* sounds when peddled, loud enough to incite riots from the neighbors who are forced to listen. And robots not only talk, they emit sirens.

Trisha's son begged for a Sesame Street Big Bird alarm clock. *Cute,* she naïvely thought as she examined the toy clock, complete with Big Bird's voice. What a great way for her son to arise from a sound sleep! Immediately upon getting home, her son unpackaged the clock and purposely moved the hands to hear Big Bird announce something like this: "Good mornnnnning! Time to wake u-uppppp! Come on, sleepy head. First the right foot, now the left. Thaaat's right. Have a nice daaaaay!"

Trisha smiled from the kitchen as she heard her son playing with the novelty clock. What a hit! When her husband came home from work, Trisha ushered him into her son's room so her little guy could show off his new clock.

Trisha, her husband, and even their older daughter thought the timekeeper was adorable until Trisha's son set the alarm for school each morning. While he became immune to Big Bird's voice, the rest of the household grimaced as the alarm recited its morning mush repeatedly and loudly. So much so, their daughter contemplated running into her little brother's bedroom to yank off Big Bird's beak.

The moral of this tip? Buyer beware. Your son gravitates toward blaring, annoying sounds. You, on the other hand, have enough noise in the house exuding from your little guy without the assistance of Big Bird or anyone else.

Alarms are meant to alarm, but we can and should choose our sirens of choice. Personally, I prefer the soothing sound of soft music. I'm sure Trisha did also. But it was too late. Big Bird had entered their home, and her only hope was for the bird to die a natural death or her son to outgrow the loud-mouthed feathered fowl.

In Trisha's words: "Today, just the thought of Big Bird's voice sends me darting toward vacant rooms in a frenzy." Hers is a familiar case of a toy coming back to haunt and taunt a mom.

Think About It. . .

♡ Grandparents enjoy buying toys for their grandsons. If you must, ask them kindly to refrain from buying the noise-toys. If they do, suggest they keep them at their house for visits. Either that or grin, give thanks, and gird up.

♡ Today's toys run the gambit. Whatever happened to simple wooden blocks or cars without roaring sounds and sirens? Chances are, even if you limit the noise-toys, your son will make his own set of sounds to correspond with his toy of choice.

FINAL THOUGHTS:

Is there anything more aggravating than a noisy toy? Yes. So don't sweat this semi-small stuff. Instead, consider that your little guy is small for a short time, even though it seems like a millennium of mischief and mayhem. So enjoy him in all of his noise-making madness. After all, he's so cute! Just like Big Bird.

51. Whenever possible, shop without your son.

It's no secret that most males dislike shopping. Their mantra? Get what you need and get out. This disdain for entering a store and actually browsing for clothes, household items, or whatever, begins early in males. It's as if they are born with a switch that activates flashing warning signs inside their brains the moment they enter a mall or department store.

Now if your child is small, no big problem. Place him in one of those cute fire engine rental strollers, give him a snack and sippy cup, and you're good to go for at least an hour or two. Unless of course he has to go to the bathroom (and he always does), or if you need to change his diaper (you always do), or if he fusses because you won't allow him to swipe every item that gets within his reach. Aside from that, your shopping experience should be tolerable.

Enter the older child. He's too old for a stroller and sippy cup. So he walks alongside you or often behind you, shuffling his feet with a rotten attitude locked firmly into place. He's the child who whines, asks repeatedly when you're leaving the mall, and makes the overall experience a nightmare.

He is notorious for both verbalizing and acting out his expressions of distain and exaggerated agony. Until you reach the toy section. Then he's all hands on deck, shelves, swords, trucks, and action figures, while begging, "Mom, can I get this?" If you reply in the negative, he breaks into an emotional outburst of disappointment and bereavement. So you toe the line and tell him, "I don't reward that kind of behavior with a toy." Well said. Of course, that's not the end of it, and you know it.

Ah yes, shopping with one's son is like carting an uncaged lion with you. And, depending on the day, he is often as scary to other shoppers as said animal would be. Potential disaster awaits when you tug along little Tommy, forcing him to shop with you. (See Tip 9.) So whenever possible, leave him in the loving arms of his dad, grandma, or friend when you have to head to the mall. No serious shopping is ever accomplished with a young son along. So why waste your time, energy, patience, and peace?

Humorist Erma Bombeck once said: "Shopping is a woman thing. It's a contact sport like football. Women enjoy the scrimmage, the noisy crowds, the danger of being trampled to death, and the ecstasy of the purchase."

Yep, we love to shop, but keep in mind your son probably doesn't. So give him what interests him while you do what interests you!

A WORD FROM THE WORD:

She considers a field and buys it.
PROVERBS 31:16 NIV

Think About It. . .

- ♡ Males are hardwired differently. Even a young daughter will enjoy shopping with mom, while a son will grimace at the mere mention of it. Adjust accordingly.

- ♡ Actress Sandra Bullock noted, "I can't selfishly take journeys anymore because I have to take a little boy along with me." Shopping is too big a journey for your son.

- ♡ Rewarding your son for good behavior while you shop is a good idea, only if he lives up to his part of the bargain. If he doesn't, don't buy the toy no matter how much he grumbles.

FINAL THOUGHTS:

You will learn as you go. A mother of a boy learns quickly how different he is from her. Her son's boisterous, inquisitive ways often frustrate and surely irritate her regularly, especially in public. So avoid the inevitable until he's able to handle the whole shopping experience. Or take along Dad, who understands his son's disinterest in the woman's sport the most. The two of them can embark on other adventures while you get your shopping done.

52. His hands are already dirty, so put them to good use.

We have pretty much established how boys love to dig, shovel, and plow through dirt. It's in their genes like running, jumping, and splashing in puddles with both feet. They are perpetual dirt magnets, and don't seem to notice or care. So put that trait into good use. Plant a garden. Yes, give him a hand shovel, seeds, and have him help you till, plant, and weed his little hands into black-dirt oblivion.

Kids love to watch plants grow. There's something about inserting a tiny seed in the ground and then watching it push through the barren soil to new life. When my kids were young, I planted a vegetable and flower garden every spring. My husband plowed the hard ground, then I marked the rows with a string, hoed an inch-deep furrow, and carefully planted the seeds.

My young sons gardened one section. They chose what they wanted to plant, and together we lunged wrist deep into new soil. Each day, they'd peer out the window to see if anything had happened yet. Before long, tiny shoots sprouted. Running inside the house, my oldest son announced, "Hey everybody, come and see!" Then he escorted the nearest family member to the window for a glimpse.

To my sons, each phase of growth was an experience—the formation of the first ear of corn, the first bean dangling from the vine, the first miniature green pepper emerging, and the first dahlia in full bloom.

Throughout the summer months, they helped me till and weed. For them, picking vegetables was the best. The rewards were not only a colorful backyard view and the taste of fresh food, but the satisfaction they received from watching the tiny seeds they planted turn into giant stalks brimming with veggies.

Gardening helps our young sons to understand and embrace the magnificence of God's creation. It garners a sense of accomplishment and teaches a solid work ethic. It gives them a sense of responsibility as they water and weed their gardens. Allowing them to plunge both hands in the soil to produce something eatable teaches them the process of growth and its rewards. Plus, gardening is fun to them.

Use gardening to teach valuable spiritual lessons to your son. For instance, God, the Master Gardener, plows the hardened ground of our hearts to plant the seed of His Word. Then He sends Christian laborers to water and weed the soil. All the while, God watches for the first sign of our spiritual growth to push through our empty souls. As the scriptures take root in our hearts, tiny sprouts of life burst through the barren soil and all things become new. Tell your son that you suspect when that happens, God escorts heaven's first available family member to the portals of paradise and exclaims, "Hurry, come and see! We have to celebrate because this brother of yours was dead and now he is alive!" (Luke 15:32).

Much like us, the Lord cultivates, weeds, and fertilizes the garden of our life, helping us to "be fruitful and increase" (Genesis 9:1 NIV), just like the scriptures explain. So let your son dig in and get dirty constructively. Besides, God, too, loves to watch things grow, especially your growing boy.

A WORD FROM THE WORD:

"Build houses and settle down;
plant gardens and eat what they produce."
JEREMIAH 29:5 NIV

Think About It. . .

♡ Don't have room for a garden? If your yard is too small or you live in an apartment, use pots to plant your son's favorites.

♡ Teach your son the joys and benefits of watching what he planted grow. Plan ahead by making a list of the vegetables he'd like to plant. Buy the seeds together.

♡ Know nothing about gardening? You're not alone. Start small. You don't need a lot of space, just some time and planning. Search the Internet for some gardening tips.

What a joy to watch your little guy grow. Watching something *he* had a hand or two in making will bring him pride, too. Give him the responsibility of watering his garden each day in the hot summer months. Gardening is a project bursting with valuable lessons and good eating.

• •

53. Appreciate the puppy dog tails before he grows lion's paws.

• •

When our sons are little, we want them to grow up. When they grow up, we long for the days when they were small. Right now your little guy radiates with snips and snails and puppy-dog tails, but soon he'll flaunt muscles, mustaches, and lion's paws.

One day my son Jeff leaned against the kitchen sink to gaze out the window. "You know, our backyard really is park-like," he said just after I read aloud the sale ad for our home: *"Apple trees, patio, and basketball post in park-like fenced backyard."*

We had just received an offer on the house, and the prospect of leaving his childhood home began to penetrate. Teenage Jeff noticed things he had taken for granted all of his life, and I was no different. For days I had reminisced the years we shared raising our two sons in the home we were about to vacate.

"You were just a little guy when we moved here, Jeff," I reminded him. "I remember when you sat at the kitchen counter and your little legs were so short they dangled from the stool." Now Jeff, six-foot-five, was too tall to even sit comfortably on the stool. My son Jimmy had been eight years old when we'd moved into this house and was now grown and married.

As flashbacks graced my mind, I could still envision Jimmy and Jeff bundled in stocking hats, snow pants, and mittens, building snowmen in the backyard. Inside, my husband would carry Jeff on his shoulders at bedtime, allowing him to push the smoke detector alarm before entering his bedroom. And Jimmy, in his G.I. Joe pajamas, would sit on the hearth in front of a blazing fire only to dart across the family room and jump on the couch to cool his heated backside. The two boys played hide-n-seek: Jeff curled beneath our leather beanbag chair while his older brother Jimmy pretended not to notice where his little brother was, despite Jeff's giggles rising from the floor.

Memories of Jimmy and Jeff playing soccer, using the chain-link fence as a goal when I wasn't looking, flooded my thoughts. I could visualize Jeff planting his own garden next to mine, the kids' rowdy basketball skirmishes, family cookouts, the boys' birthdays and open houses, Thanksgivings and Christmases, reading the Bible at the kitchen counter, and all those bedtime prayers. The house we were selling pulsated with endearing memories, and I appreciated it more than I ever had in the fifteen years we had called that house our home.

Ben Franklin said, "When the well is dry, we know the worth of water." In the hustle and bustle of raising your son, it's easy to lose sight of the memories you are creating and the fun you are having right now. Don't wait until he is grown to realize what you have in the present. Capture the little things and build on them.

Chuck Swindoll wisely noted, "Each day of our lives we make deposits in the memory banks of our children." Enjoy your son in these important years. Embrace and create memories together. Harness and appreciate his puppy-dog tails before his hands grow larger than lion's paws.

Curled up in my recliner, I scanned our former home with adoring eyes that day. "Yes, Jeff," I agreed, "we really do have a nice home. And I'm thankful for the years and memories we've had here." As I rose to leave the room, I noticed that Jeff still stared out the window. And in that moment, I somehow knew that he was thankful, too

A WORD FROM THE WORD:

And give thanks for everything to God the Father in the name of our Lord Jesus Christ.
EPHESIANS 5:20 NLT

Think About It. . .

- ♡ Appreciation is a lost art. Do you strive to attain rather than thanking God for what He helps you to maintain? Relationships, health, home, and family are all the common entities often taken for granted. Thank the Lord today for your son(s), your daughter(s), your husband, your home, and your life.

- ♡ Make memories. The little things you do with your son while he's little will bless you in the years to come. Baiting a hook may disgust you, but it will amuse your son. He'll store that memory with smiles and fondness in the years to come.

- ♡ Do you rush through activities with your son? Moms are busy, and it's hard to stop long enough to enjoy the little things. Deliberately try to slow down this week. Think of things you can do with your son: Bicycle through the neighborhood, play catch, take a walk and observe what catches his attention, or just snuggle up fireside and read a book or talk.

FINAL THOUGHTS:

J.M. Barrie said, "God gave us memories that we might have roses in December." In the springtime of your life, you seldom think about winter. You're too busy planting, watering, and working. Then December creeps in seemingly overnight, and you wonder where the time went and why you didn't spend more of it doing the things of most importance—namely, spending time with your kids and families. Cherish springtime, because winter approaches faster than you think.

54. The bully factor: Encourage him to take a stand.

Third grader John was an excellent student and a quiet boy. Mike was the class bully. He'd purposely stand behind John in line to smack him in the head when the teacher looked away. He verbally and physically assaulted the quieter, well-behaved boy whenever he could.

John's mom taught him not to settle disputes with physical violence. Besides, it just wasn't in John's personality to hit someone. So he silently and painfully endured the bullying. Then one day Mike and his friends cornered John on the playground, taking turns pushing and verbally abusing him. John wept and no one helped him.

Similar scenarios occur every day on the playground. And today there are even more resources in which bullies can harass their victims via Facebook and Twitter, and through texting and emails. Bullying is an age-old problem. Kids—especially insecure, troubled boys—prey on peers considered weaker or more vulnerable. The bully takes advantage of the weaknesses or insecurities of others, and everyone fears him because he is larger, stronger, and more aggressive than his peers. Despite detentions and past disciplinary measures, the boy continues his belligerent behavior.

Undoubtedly your son has witnessed or perhaps is the object of bullying. How does a mom deal with this problem? What should she teach her son? If a bully has ever targeted your son with acts of aggression, you know what you'd *like* to do. Just like a mother bear, you'd like to stand up on your hind legs and roar! You'd love to take the bully by the nap of the neck and resort to some bullying of your own. But, of course, it's only a passing thought. Well—ahem—maybe not passing.

In John's case, his mother approached the school's principal, but he did nothing about it. When she approached the boy's teacher, she responded, "Well, boys will be boys." It was clear that the school was unwilling to address the problem, so John's parents decided to send him elsewhere.

You are your son's best advocate at this age. Later on, your involvement might embarrass him, so it's important to teach him some common sense approaches now. Here are a few:

- ♡ **Avoid bullies and their friends as much as possible**. Stay clear of them if he can.

- ♡ **Encourage him to talk to you immediately if he's ever bullied**. Assure him that you won't take action unless absolutely necessary. He should feel free to discuss potential threats or problems with you and his dad.

- ♡ **Even though you don't condone fighting, assure your son that standing up for himself is not only acceptable but the right thing to do.** Often, that's all it takes to stop the harassment. If your son exudes self-confidence, the bully will back away. Even if your son is shaking in his sneakers, tell him to stand tall and not cower to the bully's threats.

- ♡ **If the bully's target is someone else, teach your son that it is noble and just to defend the weak or defenseless.** Instruct him to get adult help immediately, even if that means that the bully's aggression might turn toward him. Teach him to stand up for others.

Edmund Burke once said, "The only thing necessary for the triumph of evil is for good men to do nothing." No Christian mom condones fighting. But under certain circumstances it can't be avoided. Your son may get in trouble defending someone else, but applaud him for it. Boys who learn to defend the defenseless are champions of courage and strength.

Likewise, teach your son to never bully another individual. Be clear that swift and explicit consequences will result with such behavior. Today's bully is tomorrow's abusive husband and father, or con artist who derives pleasure from taking advantage of the elderly. Bullying is no small issue. Address it for what it is: wrong.

Some of the most successful men were bullied as kids. But they framed their experience in positive ways and used them as a motivator, not a terminator!

Think About It. . .

- ♡ It's hard to take a stand, but teach your son to do so when circumstances call for it. Ask him, "Would the Lord allow someone to be bullied while others just stand by and watch?"

- ♡ Is your son the object of bullying? Step in and become his advocate. Approach school authorities. Do whatever you must for the perpetrator to cease and desist.

- ♡ Don't allow bullying, and don't allow your son to bully.

- ♡ Do you think something is going on at school that your son has been afraid to tell you? Get him to talk about it and try to come to terms with what action, if any, you should take. Depending on his age, it might embarrass him for you to step in. In that case, respect that and let him work it through with your encouragement and advice.

FINAL THOUGHTS:

God defends the defenseless. He rescues the weak and needy, as should His followers. If your son is the object of bullying, don't let it go unnoticed. Likewise, instruct your son to defend others, especially those who are unable or afraid to do so themselves. Teach him that he is God's instrument and sometimes that means standing up for someone who needs his help. When he takes a stand, others will become less afraid to do so also.

55. If it smells, talks, and acts like puberty, it is.

Seemingly overnight the frightening change takes place. You are too old for adolescence and too young for menopause, so you know it's not you. No, it's your (*sniff, sniff*) little boy. Suddenly his voice cracks, he stiffens when you hug him, those yucky girls now interest him, and one whiff to his armpit seals the deal. Puberty has arrived.

How did this happen? Usually between the ages of eleven to thirteen the change comes. So you dole out the deodorant, instruct him to shower more, and brace yourself for a bumpy ride as your son slowly but surely transitions from a boy to a (*cough, sputter, hard swallow*) young man.

Mom, don't feel rejected if your once-loving son pushes you away. He's overwhelmed and he's trying to figure it all out. His body is changing. Hair has started to grow in those smelly armpits as well as on his face and other places.

Ideally, we have been introducing our sons to the "birds and the bees" at an early age. Now he's ready for the whole story to add to the bits and pieces you and your husband have conveyed over the years.

Blame it all on testosterone, that male hormone that causes such an upheaval in your son's life and in yours. That hard-wired hormone reaches its highest level during puberty, then decreases gradually after the teenage years. It infiltrates your son's body and psyche like a giant bear claw grabbing hold mercilessly. But take a deep breath, Mom. It is a God-designed transition, and happens just as the Creator intended.

But it's nice to know what to expect. So if you haven't noticed already, prepare for these changes:

- **Musculoskeletal growth.** *In other words, his once wimpy arms and legs will grow muscles and he'll soar to the heights, often towering over you.*

- **His sex organs develop.** *Enough said.*

- ♡ **Your once talkative little guy turns monosyllabic**. *He answers you with one-word replies. (See Tip 61.) And he communicates only when needed, such as asking: "Mom, what's for dinner?" or "Where's my jeans?"*

- ♡ **His interest in girls heightens faster than his stature**. *See Tips 57 and 87 for starters.*

- ♡ **His appetite increases considerably**. *The young boy you once force-fed is now the ravenous teen who searches for and finds food like a metal detector discovers coins.*

- ♡ **Ear buds or headphones become a facial feature**. *For the next seven to ten years these devices are attached to his head. So get used to the reach-and-lift motion; namely, pull out ear buds or lift up headphones before you speak to him. Music blaring, he won't hear you unless you do.*

Puberty presents surprises, like the first time you call home and your son answers the phone. "Hi, honey," you say. "When'd you get home from work?" Then you realize "honey" is your son, not your husband. Their voices sound identical now. Buying his first electric shaver is another milestone event after the peach fuzz on your son's face turns into wiry, ugly patches of hair gone wild.

Your son had testosterone from the very beginning, but now it kicks into full gear. Take a moment to gather yourself, Mom. This is just another phase in your son's ever-changing development.

A WORD FROM THE WORD:

He [God] changes times and seasons.
DANIEL 2:21 NIV

Think About It. . .

- ♡ By the way your son acts, you might think he no longer needs you. Wrong! He needs you now more than ever. Be present for him as much as possible, especially after school, at dinnertime, and at bedtime. He needs that sense of connection with you and your husband, even if he acts like he doesn't.

♡ Don't take his behavior personally. He's apt to get testy during puberty, but it really isn't about you; it's about him. Continue to love, support, and discipline him as needed.

♡ Think of ways to help your son through this transitional and often unsettling time. A part of him is still your little boy while the other part is struggling to emerge. Your understanding and love will go a long way.

FINAL THOUGHTS:

Your little boy is growing into a young man. You grieve for the past while looking forward to the future and what lies ahead for him. Puberty is a natural, normal, and necessary element to his growth. Support him, love him, and most of all pray for him (and yourself!) during this phase. Don't worry; you'll both survive.

56. To discipline is to disciple him.

It is official: Your son is a teenager, leaping from pre-adolescence to full-blown teenage boy. Inhale. It's not as bad as you think.

Typically, parents cringe at the mere thought of their son turning into a teen. You feel as if you are losing your son and gaining a monster; but don't worry, you're not. Keep the right perspective and he (and you) will not only survive, but thrive.

At this point in his development he's gravitating more toward his dad or other male role models. He's starting to make his own decisions, and that's a positive trait as long as he adheres to house rules. He still needs your supervision and guidance, Mom.

Let him know what you expect, just as you did in his earlier years. Establish consequences for inappropriate behavior and blatant disobedience. Hold him accountable. This helps to teach him responsibility while garnering a teachable spirit—which he will need even more as he matures.

After all, if he minimizes or shrugs off your instructions, he might just do the same with other authority figures, including his future employer. He may challenge your authority temporarily, but a chronic case of rebellion is unacceptable and consequences should follow. Make that clear as polished diamonds.

He may need a thumb in the back. No, he *will* need one. But just a thumb to nudge him in the right direction and keep him on track.

Yelling at him seldom produces results; rather, it generates more of the same (ugly screams, usually coming from you). Respect his privacy, allow him to voice his opinions in a respectful manner, set reasonable boundaries, and make him feel—in a culture that claws at him from all angles—that he's safe in the security of a home with parents who love and accept him.

Family expert Dr. James Dobson has written, "A boy or girl who knows that love abounds at home will not resent well-deserved punishment. One who is unloved or ignored will hate any form of discipline." Don't abandon your son now! Just because he acts like he knows what he's doing, doesn't mean he does. He might walk with a swagger, but inside he's still questioning who he is. Stick with him, Mom. He needs your understanding ear, sound advice, loving guidance, and consistent discipline.

Without disciplining your son, you may risk losing him to the world or his own foolish devices. But pick your battles. For instance: Your son wants to wear his hair long, and you detest it. But he's an honor student and a good kid. Are you going to make his hair length a huge issue?

Dobson also wrote: "Don't throw away your friendship with your teenager over behavior that has no great moral significance. There will be plenty of real issues that require you to stand like a rock. Save your big guns for those crucial confrontations."

Jesus teaches us with gentle yet firm guidance. He stands back and allows us to make mistakes. Afterward, He helps us gather the pieces of our lives that serve as lessons. Do the same with your son. Discipline him with a gentle yet firm hand; allow room for mistakes, and be there for him during his turbulent teenage years. After all, you're a major player in making him a disciple for Christ.

Think About It...

♡ Discipline begins early. If you have consistently implemented godly discipline during your son's younger years, you'll have less of struggle in his pre-teen and teenage years.

♡ Establish what your son's boundaries are and underscore the consequences of crossing those boundaries. When needed, restrict his privileges. Take away his cell phone or computer; limit his access to the television or Xbox games. Let him know ahead of time the consequences of bad behavior.

♡ Choose your battles.

♡ Loving discipline produces disciples. Talk to your son and listen equally. Guide him with God's loving-kindness.

FINAL THOUGHTS:

God disciplines His children from a heart of love. So it is with moms. If you love your teenager, you'll discipline him. Your discipline will teach him the consequences of sin and the importance of submitting to authority—characteristics everyone needs to learn to live for Christ and live successfully in this world. Like a fish out of water, your son flails with the changes going on in his body and mind. Your discipline provides your son with a sense of security and structure that every teenager craves.

57. Brace for it: The day your son grins not grimaces at girls.

Little boys cringe around their giddy counterparts. You and your husband exchange a kiss, and your small son covers his eyes and says, "Gross!" As he gets older he begins to accept girls, although he avoids having too much to do with them. If he does show a slight interest, it comes in the form of teasing a girl to gain her attention.

And then he reaches the age that terrifies you: Your son is attracted to females, big time!

These mysterious creatures called girls are fascinating to him. Now is not the time for you to back off but to get involved.

Talk about girls—how they think, feel, and act. Supply him with information about the opposite sex. Speak about your own experiences as a teenage girl and how those moments affected you. Girls are sensitive. Negative things that are said to them at a young age often linger throughout adulthood.

Despite current philosophies, girls still appreciate chivalry. A girl likes when a boy opens her car door, or gives her a hand up. (See Tip 87.) Teach your son to be a gentleman. When he goes on a date, tell him to go to the girl's door when he picks her up. When he meets her parents, though he might be shaking in his shoes, instruct him to shake her dad or mom's hand with a firm grip like he means it. Instruct him to help his date with her coat.

Inappropriate behavior or comments are unappealing to girls and just plain wrong, even if his friends think his antics are hilarious. Teach him that boys should take the lead in a relationship, but never dominate or try to control a girl.

He can learn from an expert: you! Your son has questions about girls that he may or may not feel comfortable asking you. How does he properly ask a girl for a date? What do girls like or dislike about boys? What is important to girls? He has questions (although he might not volunteer to ask), and you have answers.

If you have maintained open communication with your son while he's growing, then chances are he will receive your suggestions and advice readily. If not at first, then as time passes.

Yes, the days of your once-little son avoiding girls like the cooties is over. A new phase has begun, and God has equipped you to educate your son to become a young man who respects, honors, and values girls just as he values his mom.

A WORD FROM THE WORD:

She speaks with wisdom and faithful
instruction is on her tongue.
PROVERBS 31:26 NIV

Think About It. . .

♡ Tell your son how you felt when you were his age. Hearing about your fears, struggles, and experiences will better help him understand girls in general.

♡ Does your son approach you freely about issues with which he's concerned or confused? Listen to him without reacting. Then, more than likely, he'll feel comfortable conversing with you openly.

♡ Pray for your son as he enters his turbulent teens. These years may unnerve you, but it's less than a cakewalk for him, too.

FINAL THOUGHTS:

Author and speaker Dr. Kevin Leman said, "If you want your son to pick up how to relate to women from you rather than from sixteen-year-old Sally down the street, you have to ask yourself: Am I willing to spend as much time with him as Sally is?" Hmm.

58. Lead him to lead.

When he was little, he announced, "Everyone follow me!" as he stomped in marching style, leading you through the corridor of a museum, a school, or your home. "Come on," he said with certainty, "I'll lead the way!" You and your husband exchanged smiles as you played along. "Okay, we'll follow you!"

Your son instinctively led from the time he was small because God has hardwired males to lead, provide for, and protect their homes and families. You and your hubby raise your family together; it's a joint effort, although your roles differ. One woman stated with a grin, "My husband is the head of the home and I'm the neck. I turn him in whatever direction I like." Uh-oh. I don't think that's what God meant when He placed your guy as head of the home.

The decline of male leadership is on the rise. So what can a mom do? Let's weigh a few startling facts. More and more women have become the primary providers, caretakers, and protectors of their children as divorce rates increase. Dad has taken a back seat, whether intentionally or otherwise. Our culture stereotypes successful businessmen as aggressive, overconfident rich guys, and blue-collar workers are dubbed as sluggards whose American dream consists of a TV remote, a showcase of firearms, and a six pack of Budweiser™. Meanwhile, society ignores the hard work and determination it took for the successful businessman to achieve his goals, and the hard-working laborer toils long hours in less-than-ideal surroundings for average pay. Many husbands are men of integrity and deep moral convictions, striving to build strong marriages, raise responsible kids, and enhance their communities.

All right, after that diatribe, let's get back to your son. Dispel society's mythical and wrongful portrayal of men. Encourage your son to lead. Give him responsibilities and prompt him to take them seriously. Applaud his leadership qualities and encourage him to use them. Teach him to cultivate his relationship with Christ and, as he does, leadership traits such as honesty, integrity, a strong work ethic, responsible behavior, and maturity will emerge.

Author and pastor Rick Warren said: "Nothing happens until

someone provides leadership for it. This is a law of life."

Lead your son to lead, Mom. He already knows how, he just needs reminders. Who knows, he might just be the future president of the United States, dedicated missionary, or minister of the Gospel. But if he doesn't, he will lead by example in whatever he does.

A WORD FROM THE WORD:

Childish leaders oppress my people, and women rule over them. O my people, your leaders mislead you; they send you down the wrong road.
ISAIAH 3:12 NLT

Think About It. . .

♡ Guys are ultra-focused and task-oriented. They make great leaders. These innate abilities, along with your son's knack to compartmentalize, will serve him well in leadership positions in and out of the home.

♡ Does your son lack self-esteem? Build him up. Accentuate his strengths and minimize his weaknesses. You can keep him in line, but avoid lining him up. Society's firing squad already has their munitions aimed at him.

FINAL THOUGHTS:

You're preparing your son for his future. If you are prone to taking the lead in your home, step back and allow your husband to take charge. In your son's presence, demonstrate your love and respect for your husband. (See Tip 27.) Your man has untapped wisdom and resources with which God has equipped him. As he leads, your son will follow his example. You've heard the saying, "Live and let live"? Well, lead and let lead!

59. Tell him to shower. His family and classmates will appreciate it.

We make sure our little boys bathe, brush their teeth, and comb their hair (with our expert assistance). But as they inch from boys to men, our hands-on help is no longer welcome or appropriate. So we depend on them to groom themselves properly and manage their own personal hygiene.

Although little boys may stink of wet puppies, big boys reek of body odor, an olfactory bomb made from the combined scent of sweat, dirty clothes, and oily hair. Amazingly enough, boys tend to live as if deodorant, washing machines, and shampoo don't even exist! Why? Because teenage boys just don't care.

Since boys have a biological predisposition to smell bad, it's time for a mom intervention. If your pre-teen or teenage boy isn't showering daily, it's time to enforce some common-sense hygienic rules. Imagine sweat pouring from every conceivable body part at soccer practice or gym class. That night he goes to bed in a stinky state and returns to school the next day, smelling like he just spent a year on the city streets, living in a cardboard box.

Inform your son that no amount of antiperspirant or men's cologne will mask the nasty odor arising, like molten lava, from his pores. Good personal hygiene is in order and must be instituted immediately. Instruct him to not pass go, nor any other place, until he has washed up.

Purchase a good shampoo—especially if he has dandruff—a deodorant soap, and an antiperspirant. (Some brands have a whole selection of men's products. Buying those will make him feel like he's alpha male while giving him the initiative to actually use them.) Make sure he has a toothbrush with actual bristles and a toothpaste that he likes. Tell him those are his personal items and you expect him to use them daily.

When all else fails, be unmercifully blunt: Girls detest smelly boys. A girl is as attracted to an odiferous boy as much as she is to a box of cockroaches.

Boys should learn to implement good grooming tips early

because they will need to apply them the rest of their lives. Dirt under fingernails might seem macho to another male, but females think it's disgusting and gross. No girl, including you, wants to look at fingernails that appear as if he has just excavated an archeological site with his bare hands. Which leads us to the next suggestion. Tell him to trim his nails (finger and toes) regularly. But prepare yourself when you find fingernails and toenails scattered all over the floor. It's just your son following your advice.

And remember that Dad can always help in this area, too, although he's sure to empathize with your son a lot more than you will. Don't nag your boy, but do stress the importance of keeping it clean. Underscoring the girl issue usually seals the deal.

Stink won't keep your son from heaven, tarnish his spirit, or harm his Christian walk, but it will cause havoc in the household and alienation at school if it goes on too long without remedy. Learning good grooming and personal hygiene is all part of growing up. And who better to teach him than his mom?

A WORD FROM THE WORD:

He placed the basin between the tent of meeting and the altar and put water in it for washing, and Moses and Aaron and his sons used it to wash their hands and feet.
EXODUS 40:30–32 NIV

Think About It. . .

♡ If your son smells worse than your dog, it's time for a talk. Even your bow-wow receives proper grooming, right? So ensure that your boy is showered, shaved, and properly deodorized.

♡ Talk with your son about personal hygiene in a loving manner. You might be tempted to tease him but, instead, respect his feelings and approach him matter-of-factly.

♡ Proper hygiene practices include washing hands frequently, especially after school, playing sports, before eating, and after using the restroom.

FINAL THOUGHTS:

Comedian Jim Carrey jokingly admitted: "Ya know what I do every day? I wash. Personal hygiene is part of the package with me." Appearances are deceiving, but good grooming is essential in caring for the bodies God entrusted to us. How one presents oneself to the world matters. Your son will one day stand before a potential employer who will take your son's personal hygiene into consideration. To prepare him for that day, guide him into good grooming.

• •

60. Treat him like the kid he is.

• •

It happens all too often, especially with the eldest son of the family. Before leaving home on a business trip, your husband tells your son, "Take care of your mom and brothers and sisters. You're the man of the house while I'm gone."

"Okay, Dad, I will," your twelve-year-old son responds.

That's a typical well-intended discourse between a dad and his oldest son. And that's okay—unless your twelve-year-old son truly feels that he, alone, is responsible for his mom and his siblings.

Often parents expect their eldest son to act like an adult by giving him too much responsibility. The mom expects him to watch his younger siblings, keep the household running, and enforce rules in her absence. Occasionally that's acceptable, even good for a teenager. But when the situation becomes chronic, it poses a problem.

Have you ever met a child that, even at a young age, acted more like an adult than a child? One mother who had custody of her toddler son neglected him greatly. The small child practically raised himself. That's a modern malady. Sadly, absentee parents rely on strangers, older siblings, or electronic devices to raise their children. As a result, kids lack loving guidance and security.

Some moms make the mistake of confiding in their older son about their personal problems. The son becomes the middleman—unequipped, awkward, and uncomfortable with his involvement in his parents' marital issues. He loves them both yet he's torn, feeling the pressure to take sides. Should you have marriage problems, avoid unburdening yourself to your child. Instead, seek Christian counseling or arrange for you and your husband to talk with your pastor.

An older son isn't a human dumpster, so avoid dumping manly responsibilities or adult issues on him. To treat him as an adult is detrimental and destructive. Although a teenager, he's far from adulthood. He needs your guidance, not the other way around. Giving him age-appropriate responsibilities is healthy; but he is ill equipped to shoulder adult problems and obligations. What's more, it can become emotionally debilitating and rob him of his childhood in the long run. Allow him to be a normal kid.

Granted, today's mom has a full plate. Often we work outside as well as inside the home. We tackle packed schedules and need help. Older children are great helpers. Just remember that they're not the parents. They need the freedom to participate in school activities, sports, and social lives without the burdens that belong to you and your husband.

Evangelist Billy Graham said: "The family should be a closely knit group. The home should be a self-contained shelter of security; a kind of school where life's basic lessons are taught; and a kind of church where God is honored; a place where wholesome recreation and simple pleasures are enjoyed."

Your son doesn't need material possessions. He needs a secure home resonating with love, laughter, acceptance, and tender discipline, with you present.

A WORD FROM THE WORD:

After all, children don't provide for their parents.
Rather, parents provide for their children.
2 CORINTHIANS 12:14 NLT

Think About It. . .

♡ Older sons should have a life—their life, not their parents'.

♡ Consider how much responsibility your son shoulders. Does he watch his younger siblings daily for long periods of time? Is he expected to feed, clothe, and care for them beyond mere babysitting? Does he forego his plans because he has to help you? If the answer to any of these questions is "yes," it's time to reassess and reorganize your priorities.

FINAL THOUGHTS:

The eldest son typically feels more pressure than his siblings. He, after all, is the oldest. So a mom may often depend on him more than she should. She forgets that he's an adolescent with needs and desires of his own, apart from family responsibilities.

As the familiar axiom goes, "The squeaky wheel gets the grease." Your younger children demand more of your time and energy, so it's common to focus primarily on them. Your older son might carry his feelings inside, fearing he'll tax you more than you already are. But, in many ways, he needs you more than his younger siblings, as he faces the challenges and fears of physical and emotional growth.

• •

61. Encourage daily conversation, even when you get one-word answers.

• •

A puzzling phenomenon occurs when a boy reaches puberty. He clams up. I mean, mouth-sealed-shut-won't-talk-no-matter-what-you-ask-him clammed up. It's as if our little chatterbox turned into a mute Megatron robot overnight.

When our son is small, he asks endless questions, hardly taking a breath. He talks so much that we resort to responding to him with mindless, meaningless nods of "uh-huh" and "oh yeah." We tune him out or—at the very least—try to tune him in to some activity or video that will occupy him long enough to give our ears and minds a break.

Then, it happens. "How was school?" we ask with interest.

"Okay," he mumbles.

"Did anything new happen?"

"Nah."

"Do you have a lot of homework?"

"Not too much," he replies, using more than one word.

His three-word response encourages and delights you. *All righty, we're on a roll now!* you think, as you quickly blurt out another question to keep the "conversation" going.

Communication is vital for mothers and sons, especially as your son matures. He's going through a myriad of physical, emotional, and spiritual changes. Perhaps he's questioning his spirituality and his emerging manhood. Although Dad's input and advice are essential during this time, so are yours.

Don't discount your importance in initiating and maintaining open communication with your son, even when his responses are monosyllabic. You are the compassionate nurturer, someone with whom he can feel at ease. Listen to him and try not to overreact when he tells you something you might not like. Rather, ask him why he feels the way he does, and then be ready to give him personal and biblical illustrations to help him sort things through *without* preaching. (Ahem.)

One mom used a conversational card game to get her pre-teen to open up and talk about what was important to him. The cards asked specific questions—such as "What was the happiest day in your life?" and "What is your greatest strength and your biggest weakness?"—for each player to answer. The point of the game was to allow players to respond honestly without criticism or comment. This mom learned more about her son through that simple card game than she ever had before.

So keep in mind that specific open-ended questions (ones that cannot be answered by a simple yes or no) provoke and promote conversation. And keep talking to your son. He needs to converse with you; what's more, he wants to!

Think About It. . .

- ♡ Do you know your son's favorite sport or sports player? What's his favorite music band? Ask him about the things that interest him the most.

- ♡ If you could talk to your son about one particular thing, what would it be? Discuss it with him.

- ♡ Take time to go for a drive or a walk with your son, just the two of you. Quality time together apart from television, the social media, and all electronics promotes conversation.

FINAL THOUGHTS:

The mother-son relationship is like none other. As your son grows, make the necessary adjustments of how you treat, talk to, and address his needs. He knows he can come to you for comfort and understanding. Listen intently, pray daily, and speak to him with the love and wisdom God provides. But expect monosyllabic responses for a time.

• •

62. Monitor your pre-teen or teenager's activities.

• •

So he's a pre-teen or teenager now, and things have changed. In so many ways, you still consider him your little boy, even though he towers over you, starts his day with a morning shave, and his voice has sunk faster than a boulder in water.

As he grows, you allow him more space. You give him small doses of independence to help him learn. And although he wants to join his friends more and engage in social settings with them, your job is far from over.

Whether or not your son would ever admit it, he still needs you, although quite possibly, he'll think just the opposite. But you know better. At this stage of his development it's even more important that you monitor your son and interact with him regularly. Don't allow his propensity to hide away in his room discourage you from drawing him out. This is a vital stage in his growth, and he needs your wisdom, guidance, and sound judgment.

Chances are he won't volunteer information, so you'll have to inquire regularly. Monitor him firmly yet gently. Do you know what video games he plays or movies he sees? Is his computer in plain view, located in a common area of your home? When he goes out, do you know where he is and what he's doing? Do you have a curfew and rules for him to follow? As long as he is a minor living under your roof, you have the final word!

Lisa was a gym and health teacher at a private school. When her son was a teenager, she was teaching fourth grade health. It just so happened that at the same time she taught her students the dangers of smoking, she found cigarettes in her son's room. Immediately, she approached her son and, among other things, inquired where he bought them.

After finding out the seller's location, Lisa drove to the gas station, then confronted the female attendant who'd sold the cigarettes to Lisa's minor son. The woman denied doing so, claiming that she always asked for a photo ID. Meanwhile, a young college-age man, one of Lisa's former students, walked up to the counter for cigarettes. Immediately, the attendant asked for his ID. He chuckled as he turned to Lisa and said, "She's never done that before."

Lisa did what every mother should do. Not only did she confront her son, she confronted the store proprietor, holding her accountable. Selling cigarettes or alcohol to minors is against the law, and this mom wasn't about to let that go unnoticed or unchallenged.

Monitor your teenage son, Mom. He's under your authority and protection. He may look down on you in stance, but you tower over him in authority. God-given authority.

Think About It. . .

- ♡ As your son matures, you may think your job has reached completion. But he needs you now more than ever. Talk to him about his relationship with God, you, and others. Make yourself available to him and demonstrate your commitment to support him, but also protect and monitor his actions.

- ♡ Establish house rules. Your son needs to know what acceptable and unacceptable behavior is inside and outside of your home, and the consequences that are sure to follow.

- ♡ If you don't know who your son's friends are, find out. Get to know them.

- ♡ Hold your son accountable, but also the adults with whom he associates. If a teacher allows inappropriate behavior in a classroom, approach him or her. Should a coach do or say something that should be addressed, step up to the plate!

FINAL THOUGHTS:

Mothering teenage sons is both a joy and a job. But it need not be as arduous or terrifying as the horror stories we hear along the way. As you teach your son to follow God's Word and involve yourself in his life, you will experience less stress in his teen years. Monitoring your son is mothering him in a positive manner. He may not be your little boy anymore, but he's still your son who needs direction and guidance.

63. Plan a mother-son date.

We moms spend so much time working that we often don't spend enough quality time with our pre-teen or teenage son. Instead, we find ourselves immersed in the more laborious tasks of driving him to and from practices, meeting with teachers, laundering his clothes, cooking, and perhaps holding down a job. So our interaction with our boy is often limited to car rides and quick dinners, or those one-word conversations we discussed in Tip 61.

If this sounds familiar, then it's time to plan monthly or, better yet, weekly dates with your son. Here are a few suggestions:

- ♡ **Let him choose what to do.** Yes, this is potentially risky because he could opt to ride go-carts instead of taking your suggestion to take a "fun" walk in the woods. (Although that can be risky too. After all, his idea of a walk in the woods might be equivalent to blazing through the Amazon jungle, boring through thickets, sage brush, and brambles without a machete to clear the way.)

- ♡ **Whatever he chooses, grin and bear it.** Besides, he'll get a kick out of watching you do something totally out of your mom-box.

- ♡ **Rent a movie**. Again, let him choose it, provided it's an acceptable choice. You know he's not going to pick *The Sound of Music* or some girly movie, so be prepared. Stay up late on the weekend and watch it together—just the two of you. Dim the lights and break out bowls of popcorn. If it's a cold winter night, share some hot chocolate and swaddle yourselves in hot-out-of-the-dryer blankets.

- ♡ **If he jogs or bikes, join him!** Okay, if you aren't an exercise enthusiast, this really is a stretch (so to speak) for you. But imagine what accompanying him on a jog would do for his ego. Unless you're already a runner, jogging with him would give him the opportunity to coach his foot-shuffling, out-of-breath mom to make it around the block. Think of the tips he could share that would help you survive the trek. Biking is something everyone can do. Even if you don't travel far, he'll enjoy the time he spends with you. The bonus here is that both jogging and biking provide great exercise.

♡ **Play video and/or board games with him.** This gives your son the chance to flex his masculine muscles. Boys love to compete and love to win even more. If he's young, let him win, but if he's older, give him a challenge. Chances are he'll beat you anyway. Laugh, joke around, and have a great time.

It's amazing how much we accomplish in a day; but if we neglect spending time with our sons, we'll regret it later on. Even while you're whizzing around the kitchen, get giddy with your growing son. Stir more than the spaghetti sauce, whip up a silly song, rustle a rousing conversation, and blend some hearty laughter with frivolous fun.

Make frequent dates with him, and make sure you both keep them. Then enjoy your time together.

A WORD FROM THE WORD:

For everything there is a season,
a time for every activity under heaven.
ECCLESIASTES 3:1 NLT

Think About It. . .

♡ Channel your own childhood memories. Act crazy and silly with your son once in a while. Let loose. In the summer have hose fights drenching one another with water; in the winter go sledding with him, build a snowman, or engage in a snowball skirmish.

♡ While making dinner in the kitchen, dance with your teenage son. It doesn't matter if neither of you know how. Act silly and give it a whirl. If he's too embarrassed, stop. But if the mood is right, grab his hand and go for it! It's part of interacting on a humorous, carefree level with your teenager. (See Tip 77.)

♡ Dates are specific, planned, designated spaces of time in which you deliberately choose to interact with your son and enjoy his company. He's never too young or too old for you to "date" him.

FINAL THOUGHTS:

Remember dating your husband? You not only learned about each other, but you enjoyed one another. (Hopefully, you still do!) The same is true for your son. Taking the time to interact with your son gives both of you the opportunity to put everything and everyone else aside to simply enjoy each other's company. He finds out more about his mom, while you discover more about your son. Knowing you helps him to better understand women and girls in general.

• •

64. Remember that praise goes a long way to produce a positive self-image or result.

• •

Your son wants to please you. Whether or not you realize it, he seeks your praise and pride in him. Boys need reinforcement, and there's something you can do: Use *praise* to *produce* a *positive* self-image and/or outcome.

Sadly, many boys use anger and rebellion to act out their inhibitions, fears, or low self-esteem. Perhaps your son has an absent father and no real positive male role model. Or his attempt to please his dad, you, or others goes unnoticed. Over time, these issues take their toll and behavioral problems arise. Just as a girl seeks love and attention, a boy seeks admiration and respect.

When my eldest son was fifteen years old, he sat at our kitchen counter as I made dinner. I was in a bad mood and he knew it. Whenever I'd get in one of my funks, he thought it had something to do with him.

"What's wrong, Mom?" he asked.

"Nothing!" I snapped.

Gingerly, he asked, "Mom, did I do something wrong?"

I'd typically answer with an abrupt, "No," and continue what I was doing, leaving him disheartened and even feeling guilty for something he never did. But on this particular day, God revealed what I was actually doing. The Holy Spirit spoke to my heart, *"You're doing to your son exactly what your grandmother did to your father."* My grandmother, who'd had four sons was, sadly, the travel agent for guilt trips. To think I had opened my own travel agency hit me with the force of a ten-foot wave.

Instantly, I turned to my son and explained that my mood had absolutely nothing to do with him and everything to do with me. I reinforced what a good son he was and that, although I appreciated his sensitivity to my awful moods, he wasn't the cause of them. From that day on, I never responded to him like that again. Rather, I endeavored to use my words to uplift, not disparage him.

If your son makes an attempt to do something you suggested, praise him for it. If he accomplishes a goal or overcomes a fear, voice how proud you are of him. Reward him with his favorite dessert or dinner. Boys want to achieve, and they feel like failures far too much. Sensitive moms zero in on those times to bolster their boy's self-worth and self-esteem.

This begins early. Ask your six-year-old son to open a jar for you and watch his response. He'll dash to your side to assist you. Although he may spill the jar's contents all over the floor, thank him for being mommy's little helper! (See Tip 25 and Tip 41.)

Praise produces positive results in our sons. Our words have the power to help or harm them. So remember what all boys need: Praise to produce the positive in their life.

A WORD FROM THE WORD:

Wise words satisfy like a good meal;
the right words bring satisfaction.
PROVERBS 18:20 NLT

Think About It. . .

♡ Your heavenly Father is an encourager. His words breathe life into His people. God calls every mother to encourage, praise, and uplift her son with His life-giving words. A mom does that through positive reinforcement of who her son is and what he can accomplish with her encouragement and God's Spirit to guide him.

♡ Think of ways you may have disheartened your son. Ask his forgiveness and commit to practice praising him.

♡ Did your son accomplish something new today? Give him a hug wrapped in positive reinforcement.

FINAL THOUGHTS:

The boys who are the recipients of constant teasing, degrading, or critical and embarrassing comments are the sons who become beaten-down, angry men. To them, harsh criticism equates to failure, and failure equals inadequacy. Moms have the power to deter catastrophic consequences and reinforce their sons simply through consistent acknowledgement of their accomplishments. Who doesn't enjoy a pat on the back? Give one to your son today.

65. Boys don't hear you. So get to the point.

Women are emotional. Our passions run deep. Our thoughts run simultaneously in five different directions. We have tons to say and we usually say it. Boys, on the other hand, disdain details; they are sight and sound oriented. They respond to noise, visual stimulation, and physical contact. That explains why blaring, action-oriented video games and contact sports draw them like an 80 percent discount lures females to the mall. But listening is not a male's strength; neither is talking at any great length, unless it's something of intense interest to them. As they mature, they become more nonverbal. (See Tip 61.) For example:

"Jay, turn down your music."
Silence.
"Did you hear me, Jay? I said, turn it down!"
More silence; music blaring.
"That's it! Turn that thing off!"
He finally answers. "What'd you say?"
"You heard me, I told you to turn that thing off!" The problem is, he really didn't hear you. He was so focused on what he was doing that he mentally shut down everything and everyone else around him.

So how do we get him to listen? Keep it short and simple. Your son *expects* long dissertations from you. If you tell him you'd like to talk, he knows he's in for a lengthy gab session (with all the gabbing done on your part). So discuss, not overdiscuss, or you'll lose him.

Unlike daughters, sons accept short directives pretty well. While a daughter may question why she has to take out the garbage, and why the family makes so much garbage, and besides that it's stinky and yucky, and it really is a boy's job to do, a son responds better when you stick to the point. If you approach your son with calm directives he'll listen far better than if you hysterically rant in total frustration, saying something like: "Jay, take out the garbage now, because the last time I asked you, you forgot and then I heard the garbage truck outside and I had to scramble to tie up the garbage before I missed taking the cans to the curb like you were supposed to do!"

Keep in mind that boys are visual, so yes, have him turn off the music, TV, Xbox game, iPad, or whatever else captures his undivided attention. Then look him in the eye and tell him in short sound bites what you wish to convey. "Jay, please take out the garbage *now*." Period, end of story. If you must, use your facial expressions. You know, the motherly glare that speaks louder than words? (See Tip 45.)

Remember that talk—lengthy gab session—I mentioned earlier? Mere minutes pass before you notice his glazed-over expressions of disinterest. He tolerates you, but he's not listening. So be brief and get to the point. You might try to interject a personal illustration to kindle his interest or ask his opinion. And then he might just listen, but only briefly.

A WORD FROM THE WORD:

Do not be quick with your mouth, do not be hasty in your heart to utter anything before God. God is in heaven and you are on earth, so let your words be few.
ECCLESIASTES 5:2 NIV

Think About It. . .

♡ Are you a droner—a mom who verbalizes everything from what you bought at the mall to how frustrated you were with the sales clerk? Do you talk to your son and hear little if any response? Chances are, he's already tuned you out.

♡ Achieve eye contact when you talk to your son. Don't mince words and stay on point.

♡ Remove all forms of distraction when you talk with him.

Boys want to know what you expect and what you want in simple, easy-to-read-you instructions. Avoid too many details, unless he inquires or show interest. A television series in the 1960s featured a detective who, at the crime scene, usually encountered a chatty woman who gave every minute detail of what she witnessed. The detective was famous for saying, "Facts. Just the facts, ma'am." Good advice.

66. Accept it: Boys gravitate toward the gross side of humor.

He bellows a belch and breaks into laughter. Gastrointestinal sounds are music to his ears. Tween and teen boys find humor in the disgusting. Their competitive nature turns silly as your son and his friends have a contest to see who can burp the loudest or the most consecutive times. Expelling gas is hilarious to him, especially when eliminated at awkward moments. Making fart sounds with his hands is a timeless trick sure to bring hearty guffaws among his like-minded peers.

Face it. Potty issues, embarrassing moments, and over-the-top silliness fascinate boys. They thrive on practical jokes and embarrassing pranks. A boy finds it especially amusing to prank his sister or mom because what boys deem hilarious, girls think "gross!" And boys *love* to taunt.

One little boy decided to put catnip on the back of his grandmother's robe so his cat would jump up and nip his grandma's bottom. It worked great, and he and his grandma had a good laugh together. (Thank God for grandmas with a sense of humor.)

Accept the fact that your son thinks that anything gross is entertaining and side-splitting. Fake puke is an essential tool for pranks, as are rubber slimy worms and life-like insects or reptiles. To find a fake worm in your Jell-O mold is to be the mother of a fun-loving, mischievous son.

As your son matures, his sense of humor may temper. Yet some boys grow to adulthood, maintaining the same level of gross humor that they bellowed and enjoyed as a teenager. That gets old if taken too far! Actor Mickey Rooney admitted: "I was a thirteen-year-old boy for thirty years." Yes, for some boys, finding amusement in the indelicate is intrinsic and lingers long. But a wise, tuned-in mom can help the tempering process along.

Boys just like to have fun, even if it's at the expense of their unwary sibling or weary mom. Lighthearted pranks and jokes are normal, even if you shake your head in dismay. But if and when the jokes become harmful, inappropriate, reflect poor manners, or border on bullying, step in and discuss your boy's propensity for finding amusement derived from unsuitable behavior at the expense of others. Administer proper discipline and consequences for unsuitable, misplaced humor.

Otherwise, allow your son to be a boy. The sooner you accept that his disgusting humor is just part of his nature, the sooner you'll relax and let his antics roll off your back. Unless, of course, you must first detach the cat from your backside.

A WORD FROM THE WORD:

Folly is bound up in the heart of a child.
PROVERBS 22:15 NIV

Think About It. . .

- ♡ Is your son a prankster? Just make sure he doesn't take his humor too far.

- ♡ A healthy sense of humor is a must-have for every individual. Allow your boy to express his silliness and foolishness. If he doesn't now, he will later on when it's not so funny anymore.

- ♡ Laugh with him. You needn't encourage his boy-humor, but you can force a smile, right?

FINAL THOUGHTS:

Okay, so your son's humor is annoying. His dad snickers while you roll your eyes. You don't have to agree with his gross sense of humor, but you can accept it if it is exercised in moderation. Too much of anything is too much.

• •

67. Hug him often or as much as he'll let you.

• •

Hugging your son begins immediately at birth and extends throughout his lifetime. It's an ongoing act of love and affection, a nonverbal expression of how much he means to you. From his first fall to his first day of college, ample hugs administered at appropriate times communicate support, comfort, and understanding.

Showing frequent displays of outward affection give your son a sense of security and belonging. Of course, an adolescent boy will shun any display of affection in public, so avoid doing so in the presence of others if he's uncomfortable. And rare is the teen who *is* comfortable. So spare him embarrassment and probable teasing from his friends and save your hugs for when he's away from the peering of his peers.

Michele, mother of three boys, said that hugs in her home are common. If a sibling argument turns combative, she taught the offenders to hug one another while offering apologies. "You can't stay mad very long after a hug," she quipped. "We are a hugging family. In our home, hugs are given consistently and liberally!"

Have you ever known someone who has suffered a personal loss? A simple hug is enough to soothe and comfort them. If your son injures himself, hugs seem to mend the wound faster. And a shoulder hug to a disappointed goalie after a tough soccer game, says, "Don't worry; you'll do better next time."

Some data claims that hugs, like laughter, produce medical benefits such as lowered blood pressure, reduced heart rates, increased nerve activity, and are a catalyst to improve overall moods.

One report suggests that when a person is hugged, his comfort level increases. A hug is a noncommunicative action that awakens happy memories and helps a person feel acceptance without saying a word. It eases our minds and bolsters our spirits. If a genuine, heartfelt hug can do that for us, imagine what it does for our growing sons?

Each day your son's self-esteem is tested as he competes for acceptance and approval. Pre-teens and teenager boys tote insecurity like we tote handbags, though our sons would never admit it; rather, they hide their insecurities. That's why hugs are the medicine they need and—despite how it appears—they want.

It's been said that "a mom's hug lasts long after she lets go." So don't underestimate the power of your hugs, Mom. It's the gift that keeps on giving and receiving. After all, what mom doesn't melt in the arms of her loving son, no matter his age? Hugs are a priceless commodity readily accepted and appreciated.

A WORD FROM THE WORD:

May the Lord lead your hearts into a full understanding and expression of the love of God.
2 THESSALONIANS 3:5 NLT

Think About It. . .

♥ The familiar bumper sticker, Have you hugged your kid today? asks a valid, thought-provoking question designed to produce results. So have you? If not, go hug him right now, just because.

♥ If your son isn't used to outward displays of affection, begin slowly and don't force him. But think about this: If he feels awkward hugging you, chances are he'll feel uncomfortable showing his future wife outward expressions of love, too.

♥ Did you grow up in a home void of outward displays of affection? You can change that in your home beginning with your husband and children. Boys often grunt in disgust when mom and dad kiss or hug in their presence. But don't be deceived. You and your spouse's appropriate displays of affection for one another assures your son that his home life is secure.

FINAL THOUGHTS:

Hugging your son causes a positive ripple effect. The act prepares him to interact with friends and family members more readily, without embarrassment or feelings of awkwardness. Teach your son that hugging isn't just for women! Men embracing one another from a heart of friendship, brotherhood, and Christian faith is a beautiful thing.

68. Set boundaries.

Your boy is diving into the world headfirst. He wants independence, but despite his claims, you know that he can only handle it in well-measured increments. So the need to establish boundaries will help him, and you, as he grows.

But what is the definition of *boundaries* anyway? Why are they so important? How do we implement them in our son's life? One book defines personal boundaries as "guidelines, rules or limits that a person creates to identify for him or herself what are reasonable, safe and permissible ways for other people to behave around him or her and how he or she will respond when someone steps outside of those limits. They are built out of a mix of beliefs, opinions, attitudes, past experiences and social learning." Whew, in simpler terms, setting boundaries is the simple act of establishing rules and order in the home and then maintaining them.

Imagine a world without rules or boundaries. About now you might think: *I live in that world daily. It's called controlled chaos.* But consider this. God issued the Ten Commandments to establish tranquility, structure, and order. That's why rules are important. If we run a stoplight or refuse to wear a seat belt, consequences follow. Boundaries are set in the classroom and the workplace, so why not at home, life's training ground where you and your family spend the most time?

At this stage of your son's life, the lines blur and he needs to know beforehand what his boundaries are. What should he expect of you? What do you expect of him? No sudden surprises, please. Talk with your husband about what's acceptable and unaccept-able for your son. With a united front, discuss these boundaries with your son.

Here are some things to consider: What's his curfew? How long will you allow him to grow his hair? How many sports can he participate in during the school year? What type of behavior won't be tolerated? What kind of movies or video games can he watch or play? What school grades do you expect? Is he allowed to use Facebook or Twitter?

Assure him that you're not his dictator but his facilitator and greatest advocate. God placed parents in the role of guiding, loving, and disciplining their kids. As you allow age-appropriate levels of freedom for your son to make his own decisions, he will begin to build his own boundaries as he matures.

Meanwhile, we need to model our personal boundaries before our son. Let's face it, if our personal expectations are low and our boundaries waver like a staggering drunk, what can we expect from our son? Hmm, perhaps a whole lot of the same injected with a hardy dose of *un*controlled chaos?

A WORD FROM THE WORD:

We will not boast about things done outside our area of authority. We will boast only about what has happened within the boundaries of the work God has given us, which includes our working with you.
2 CORINTHIANS 10:13 NLT

Think About It. . .

♥ In His Word, God establishes clear-cut boundaries for us to follow. Explain to your son that God never intended to spoil his fun, rather to protect, guide, and help him. "The wages of sin is death"(Romans 6:23 NLT) and destruction is the end result of sinful, out-of-control lifestyles and behavior.

♡ Remember, boundaries are love in action. If you love your son, you will set limits and lovingly discipline him when he oversteps them.

♡ If your son improves his grades, obeys the rules, or adheres to the guidelines you've set, reward him. Surprise him with something special to encourage his positive behavior and active cooperation.

♡ Ask your son what he thinks are reasonable boundaries for his age. Listen to his ideas, but make it clear that the final authority lies in your court.

FINAL THOUGHTS:

Have you ever overstepped your boundaries? Not a great feeling. When your son does, don't lather on the guilt. He already feels plenty. Firmly and gently support him while helping him to learn from his mistakes.

69. Take a deep breath, then discuss sex and dating.

Does this tip cause you immediate discomfort? Would you rather tread barefoot on barbed wire than approach this subject with your son? Then take your place in a very long line of other parents on the brink of approaching "the talk."

Every mom winces when her little boy sprouts into adolescence and all that entails. But don't wince too much, because he needs your advice and counsel. Shelve your personal embarrassment, collect your thoughts, take a chill pill, and yes. . .talk to him.

Ideally, this is dad's domain, and your husband is better suited to approach the subject with your son. Regardless, you play an important role in this area of education, too. So you've been through a brief, watered-down version of the how-babies-are-made talk some time ago, but now he knows—or needs to know—the nitty-gritty of it all. If you and/or your husband have addressed the issue early and openly with your son, by the time he reaches puberty he will have a somewhat clear—with only a few scattered, overcast clouds—understanding of sex. Take another breath, Mom. Okay, let's continue.

Boys feel awkward, unsure of how to act with a girl. Tell him. Teach him how to make life choices and instruct him to set personal boundaries for himself, long before a first date. Underscore the fact that it isn't just the girl's job to say "no." If he waits for that moment of heated passion, then he's waited too long. Perhaps he can initiate making a pact with his like-minded friends to abstain from sex before marriage. In doing so, they hold each other accountable and create a support system.

His hormones are raging with testosterone levels at an all-time high. Instruct him that God gives us a free will, and he has a choice. Animals are animals and he's not one of them, no matter what some textbooks tell him. Explain to him that God's Word is clear about sex before marriage and the consequences of such actions. To obey God means for your son to maintain his purity, and purity isn't just for girls! God calls males to the same standards recorded in His Word.

Boys should respect and value their bodies and avoid sexual temptations. Likewise, they should understand that girls aren't mere physical objects to use and then dispose of. Pornography degrades women and desensitizes boys' perception of them. Warn him of its dangers. How he views girls and the level of respect he gives them is significant when he's choosing his future wife.

Many teenagers begin dating too soon. Doing so is like riding a roller coaster. At first, the thrill of the ride is enough. Soon the smaller version doesn't satisfy anymore and he seeks roller coasters that reach greater heights at faster speeds. Similarly, at first a kiss is enough, but the more often and longer he dates, the more he desires. According to experts like Dr. James Dobson, it stands to reason that the longer your son delays dating, the greater chance he'll have of remaining sexually pure.

Too much too soon is dangerously unwise. So is the assumption that your son can handle the sexual tensions and temptations associated with dating early. Encourage group dates or outings rather than dating apart from his peers.

The pursuit of sex before marriage destroys. Self-control and respect for oneself and for others blesses. Uh-oh, I think it's time; you're next in line! Still breathing?

A WORD FROM THE WORD:

Flee from sexual immorality. All other sins
a person commits are outside the body,
but whoever sins sexually, sins against their own body.
1 CORINTHIANS 6:18 NIV

Think About It...

♡ Open God's Word and read scriptures pertaining to sexual immorality. Discuss together what the verses mean.

♡ Talk about the consequences of premarital sex: unwanted pregnancies (premature but permanent fatherhood); incurable sexually transmitted diseases; a propensity toward promiscuity; unhealthy, destructive relationships; damaged lives and more.

♡ Unfortunately, society's prevailing attitude is that teenage boys will have sex despite what parents do. The world may accept that as the norm, but Christians know better. Talk to your son about sex and dating. Pray for him daily.

♡ Does your teenage son believe the myth that manhood means having premarital sex? Dispel the myth. Teach him that it takes a bigger man to say no to sex than it does to say yes.

♡ Underscore the fact that, despite society's claims, there is no such thing as "safe sex."

FINAL THOUGHTS:

Although movies and television programs bombard boys with images and messages that feature macho men jumping from one partner to another, moms know that a real man exhibits self-control and self-discipline. God is able to help your son remain pure throughout his teenage years into adulthood. Keep the communication lines open at all times. Discuss sex and dating without pressure or criticism. If he knows he can turn to you, he's less likely to make poor decisions that can negatively alter his life.

• •

70. Noise comes with boys, so invest in earplugs.

• •

You've known it for a long time. Boys should come with a warning label at birth: Warning: This Boy Comes with Noise. Almost before you know it, his infant cries turn into shouts of "woof, woof" with high-fives a blazin' and fist bumps a poundin'. Gather a group of guys together and booming voices and grunt-like utterances emerge in a cacophony of unusual boisterous sounds.

Big and little boys alike enjoy making noise ranging from fabricating roars as they whisk their toy car or to revving their car engines in their teenage years. Action figures soar, jump, and spin complete with verbalized explosions.

During my sons' teenage years, summer vacation went fine until about three weeks before school began. That was when I typically underwent a personality change brought on from having two boys home *all* day, *every* day. I'd begin gnashing my teeth and counting to ten as my kids' behavior gnawed at me like hungry termites feasting on rotted wood. Petty annoyances seemed like aggravated assaults on my well-being; sibling arguments turned into major warfare, and normal noise levels evolved into exaggerated explosions.

My one son in particular thumped around the house like a monkey bouncing from one surface to another. Whatever he did, he did *loudly*. Lids, drawers, and doors were not merely closed; they were banged shut. *Clang. Boom.* I'd wince. "Jeff, take it easy!"

"What?" he'd reply. (*What* in teenage-boy language means, "I didn't do anything wrong so you figure out what 'what' means.")

"You know what. Stop slamming doors," I'd say in my most authoritative voice.

"I'm just getting a glass," he'd counter.

"I knoooow, Jeff," I'd bellow. "Just quit making such a racket!"

"What?" (There's that word again.)

"Jeff, I can't concentrate when you're banging around the house!"

With a look of disgust, he'd leave the room as I tugged at my hair and reached for the calendar. "Three more weeks and the house will be *mine, mine, mine* again," I'd mutter.

Some noises are soothing and uplifting like the sound of waves crashing against the shore. The Bible instructs us to make a joyful noise praising the Lord. And there's nothing more edifying than the sound of Christian music as God's people lift their hearts and voices to God.

But boy noise is, well, noisy to the sensitive feminine ear. So although our sons don't make noise all the time (though it may seem like it), when they do we either have to accept it, try to reduce it to an inside-voice decibel (a constant battle), or invest in ear plugs.

That said, believe it or not (don't tune me out here), one day after he's grown and gone, you'll actually miss the sights and sounds of your raucous son. What? There's that word again!

A WORD FROM THE WORD:

No one could distinguish the sound of the shouts of joy from the sound of weeping, because the people made so much noise. And the sound was heard far away.

EZRA 3:13 NIV

Think About It. . .

♡ Much like the above scripture, moms often aren't sure what the household hubbub is all about. Are the kids fighting or just playing? Distinguish bad noise (arguing and fighting) from good noise (joking, laughing, and playing). Their "good noise" should become white sound to you—a welcomed clamor in your home.

♡ Noise is normal in average households, but when your son's racket rises above the threshold of your noise limits, put a limit on him. Teach him that there is a time for noise and a time for silence. And now is the time for silence.

FINAL THOUGHTS:

Boys come with noise, but they also bring moms a lot of joy. Focus on the positive qualities your son brings to your home and life. Embrace your son's normal, masculine traits and underscore his talents and potential. After all, boys come with noise, but that's not what they're all about.

• •

71. Help him find his niche.

• •

Boys have similar characteristics, but they are unique individuals. For instance, we assume that all boys enjoy playing sports. But your son may dislike sports, much to the disapproval of his football-watching-basketball-playing dad. (See Tip 33.) Your son's disliking stereotypical boy activities doesn't make him inferior or effeminate, it just makes him an individual with dissimilar interests from his parents and some other boys.

If he bounces the basketball with deliberate imprecision, or attempts to kick the soccer ball, misses, and hits his dad's ankle instead, don't search the Internet for answers to your son's lack of athletic prowess. Rather, encourage him in the activities he does enjoy and is good at.

Seventeen-year-old Ian is a self-ascribed nerd. He loves books. He began reading at the impressive age of four. Even at seven months old, Ian would stare at the pictures while his mom read to him. Either that or she mistakenly *thought* he was concentrating on the pictures while he was really nodding off to sleep. Regardless, he enjoys reading, learning, and visiting museums and science exhibits. He is a human sponge who can't glean enough knowledge. Today he has aspirations to become a physician.

Ian tried sports but felt as comfortable on a soccer field as most of us feel sequestered in a room with a rodent. Although he engages in other boy-like activities, his favorite thing to do is read, read, and read. Every mother's dream!

Mom, help your son find his niche. Encourage his proclivity to play the piano or a game of chess, or take an art class instead of watching the Chicago Bulls (do you hear a collective gasp from all dads?). He is an individual, with God-given gifts and abilities, some of which have nothing to do with athletics, riding roller coasters, or race car driving (thank God).

Allow your boy to be himself without pressuring him to engage in the activities you or your husband like to do, or think he should do. Likewise, if your son loves football or wrestling and you squirm at the thought of him playing a sport that could potentially hurt him, ease into it and let him try. If not, you'll regret holding him back from something he loves to do.

Accept him for who he is. Ralph Waldo Emerson said: "To be yourself in a world that is constantly trying to make you something else is the greatest accomplishment."

Moms are their sons' greatest advocates. We stand our ground to defend them, we encourage and equip them, we love them unconditionally, and we help them find their niche in life because we desire for them to flourish, grow, and use the gifts God has entrusted to them.

A WORD FROM THE WORD:

In his grace, God has given us different gifts for doing certain things well.
ROMANS 12:6 NLT

Think About It. . .

♡ Sports are overrated. Have you ever heard someone talk

about a successful man's accomplishments? Unless he is a world-class athlete, no one ever remembers or cares that he was a jock in high school! Although sports teach boys a host of valuable life lessons, being an athlete isn't the end all.

♡ What does your son enjoy doing? Present him with the resources he needs to pursue his interests. Take family field trips to places your son likes. If your children's interests differ (and they probably will), then alternate trips so everyone gets a turn at going to or doing what they enjoy most. In that way, everyone will learn to take turns and engage in other activities they'd normally avoid.

♡ Are there other "team" efforts your son might like? Consider his participation in his school's debate team or joining a noteworthy organization or club.

FINAL WORD:

Your son is special. (Of course you know that already.) Although boys share a lot of generalities, they have individual personalities, abilities, interests, and goals. While one son whoops and hollers, another is more studious and introverted, preferring a quiet corner in which to read. Help your son hone the qualities that are uniquely his own. By all means, avoid unnecessary assumptions if your son doesn't fit society's idea of what a boy should do, be, and act like. Remember, today's nerds are often tomorrow's neurosurgeons.

• •

72. Promote common sense. Your teen may lack in that department.

• •

A weekend getaway with your husband sounds inviting. Deciding what to do with your teenage son, however, is the big issue. Do you ship him to his grandparent's house or. . .?

"Please, Mom," your son begs, "I'll be fine by myself. You can trust me."

It's not that you don't trust him. It's just that, even without meaning to, teenagers can easily transform into lethal weapons when left to their own devices.

René Descartes said, "Common sense is the most widely shared commodity in the world, for every man is convinced that he is well supplied with it." And every teenage boy thinks he is, too.

My once-teenage son thought he was heavily endowed with common sense and often tried to assure us that we could leave him alone overnight. Yet here was a kid who, when sent to the store for a bag of potatoes, returned with zip, zero, nothing.

"Where are the potatoes?" I questioned, as he entered the door bag-less.

"I looked, but they didn't have any," he answered in a tone hinting of desperation.

"What do mean they didn't have potatoes?" I countered. "Grocery stores always *have* potatoes."

"Well," he explained, "I looked everywhere for the white potatoes you wanted, and all they had were Idaho."

This is the same teen who expected us to unreservedly abandon our parental judgment and leave him alone overnight? One thing most teenage boys definitely lack is common sense. We can teach them some things, but the must-have trait of common sense is acquired over time.

Throughout our sons' growing up years, we moms try to instill tidbits of wisdom we are certain they won't learn from a textbook. We pass on gems such as: Look both ways before crossing the street. Don't talk to strangers. Keep your cell phone charged and on when you're away, and respond when I text you. Share and be fair. Never wait until bedtime to tell me to launder a uniform, bake a cookie, or hand me progress reports.

These are simple, common sense rules that make life a lot easier. But do teens listen? Sometimes, rarely, or not at all. Any three can and will apply in various and sundry situations.

Like our heavenly Father does with us, moms must enforce, teach, love, and guide our sons into the wonderful realm of common-sense thinking. The question is, after fifteen, sixteen, or seventeen years, has your son internalized the lessons you have taught him? Have you sown enough common-sense seeds into His heart to comfortably entrust him with more responsibility? Hmm, could it be that God, too, ponders similar questions about His kids?

Think About It. . .

♡ Ask yourself: When an uncontrollable burst of adolescent absurdity strikes, can you trust your son to handle the situation without your supervision?

♡ Give him some slack where and when you can safely do so to test the waters of his independence; keep a closer rein when you know better.

♡ It's possible for your son to be book smart yet common sense deficient.

FINAL THOUGHTS:

All moms desire their sons to become men of discernment and wisdom, but that takes time, effort, and experience in the classroom of common sense. Your son might have Einstein's intelligence, but if he lacks Solomon's common-sense wisdom, what good is it? Maybe that's why the Lord instructs us, throughout the scriptures, to seek wisdom. It just makes good common sense!

73. Hand him twenty bucks and teach him fiscal responsibility.

Your son thinks—as the familiar adage goes—that "money grows on trees." So he knows you and/or your husband work to pay the bills because that's what he heard you or someone else say. But don't expect him to understand, appreciate, or grasp in any way, shape, or form, fiscal responsibility. (Hey, if the federal government doesn't get it, how can we expect a fourteen-year-old boy? Huh?)

After you escort your son into the backyard to prove money trees don't exist, talk real world scenarios. If he wants a cell phone, iPad, computer, or any other technological money-grabbing gadget, teach him the importance of budgeting. If he receives an allowance, have him record what he spends in one week. Listing items with corresponding amounts will give him an indicator of just how much he really spends, or how much he needs. Then help him budget his money to purchase what he wants.

Doing so helps him to set goals. He may pester you for a cell phone with all of the reasonable yet not-so-valid arguments, but does he realize that maintaining the phone will cost you money every month? Consider having him pay a small portion of the bill. Although his meager pittance may not help you much, it speaks volumes to him, namely, "Hey, this cell phone plan costs a lot more than the phone itself."

Teach him how to save money. He already knows how to spend it. If you teach him early, you might just spare him some hard financial knocks in the future. When he receives money for his birthday or Christmas, encourage him to save a portion of it. Open a joint bank account if that seems reasonable to you, so he can place monies directly into his account. Or place his money in a money market that gleans more interest. He'll love watching his cash accumulate over time, and it will give him a sense of accomplishment.

From the get-go, teach him to tithe. To put God first in everything is to give to His work immediately, not if and when your son has money left over. Learning to give to God first is like learning to brush your teeth before leaving the house in the morning. It should become routine. Don't know where to start? Hand your son a twenty-dollar bill and tell him that this is the beginning of his learning how to manage his money. Tell him that he has to budget his money for the next two weeks, using the money to buy what he needs. Allow him to make mistakes. Undoubtedly, he'll spend it swiftly. Then when it's gone and he wants more for whatever, tell him he already spent his money. Explain the lessons of saving and spending cash and help him implement them.

If you disagree with giving a weekly allowance, give him projects or work to do to earn cash. Encourage him to shovel sidewalks in winter months or mow lawns in the summer for extra income. This teaches your son the value of money and just how hard it is to come by!

Instruct him about the dangers of debt. It's like a giant sinkhole, sucking in everything you have. Just about the time you think you've grabbed the top to climb out, another unexpected expense swallows you.

Someone once said, "The only man who sticks closer to you in adversity than a friend is a creditor."

Owing money strangles; owning money frees. Teach and lead your son to borrow infrequently, save consistently, and give generously.

A WORD FROM THE WORD:

Good planning and hard work lead to prosperity,
but hasty shortcuts lead to poverty.
PROVERBS 21:5 NLT

Think About It. . .

♡ Does your son think that money magically comes from an ATM machine? Does he expect one touch of a button to supply a steady flow of cash to accommodate all of his desires? Then it's time to inject a dose of reality about wise spending habits.

♡ Money management should begin early. If you dole out cash like candy on Halloween the moment your son wants something, he'll expect to get what he wants, when he wants it, from now until he reaches middle-age or beyond.

♡ Make saving fun. Start a family money fund to save for vacations or household items everyone can enjoy. Encourage your son to contribute. Have a sign-in sheet so family members can record what and when they gave.

FINAL THOUGHTS:

Because kids learn through their parent's example, your spending habits will pass on to them. (*Cringe.*) Do you pay your bills on time? Are you an impulse buyer? Do you give liberally? Remember: Your son is watching every move you make. So why not underscore the value of money management and exercise the discipline of self-control? In doing so, you will establish biblical financial concepts in him that he will hopefully carry into adulthood.

• •

74. Engage in some payback time with your teen to teach him that the world doesn't revolve around him.

• •

When my husband and I first took clogging lessons (the tap-shoes, aerobic version of line dancing), we announced to our then teenage sons that we expected them to attend our clogging graduation party at the end of our first six weeks.

Their jaws dropped and they became mute. With blank stares they stood side by side, retaining a catatonic stance for several minutes before our eldest son spoke. "Jeff," he said, turning to his brother who appeared as if he had just been given a lethal injection, "they're getting back at us for all of the sporting events they had to attend over the years."

He was partly right. Raising two athletic boys was an endless replay of *Wide World of Sports*. All of those little league baseball games, track and cross-country meets, and basketball and soccer skirmishes were embedded in my mind like grass stains on white sweat pants. I can still sense the thrill of sitting on dusty park bleachers in 95-degree heat, anticipating that fleeting moment when, with bat in hand, our little slugger stepped up to the plate.

Ah yes, and those soccer games: The opportunity to relax in a lawn chair while struggling with blankets and an unbridled umbrella to repel the cold pelting rain and whipping wind. And how could we forget the rush we received while pushing through the crowd with one eye on the stopwatch and the other on our cross-country runner as he reached the two-and three-mile splits? What an opportunity for personal growth we embraced while crammed between screaming parents in an overheated gymnasium to cheer on our home-grown version of Michael Jordan.

The stench of dirty tube socks and grimy uniforms, and the task of scraping mud—of concrete consistency—from the bottom of soccer shoes made our sports experiences complete. And what a reward it was to stay up late to launder basketball jerseys or baseball uniforms because one of our sons waited until bedtime to tell me he needed it the next day.

To all of this, add the guilt factor. You know, that gnawing feeling that occurs when you miss a few games or secretly hope your son's team will lose a tournament game to shorten the lengthy basketball season?

Nope, I never cared much for sports until I birthed two sons who did. Suddenly, it didn't matter if my sons' games disrupted my schedule or if my back ached from sitting for hours on hard wooden benches. I tolerated it all because I'm their mom.

Johann Wolfgang von Goethe said, "We are shaped and fashioned by what we love." Your son shapes your interests anew. If he enjoys playing musical instruments, you encourage his efforts, listen to his practice sessions (sometimes with earplugs), and attend every recital with pride. If he likes a certain sport, you become a fan of that sport. If he enjoys reading, you support him with regular trips to the bookstore. If he likes photography, you buy him what he needs to pursue his hobby.

Yes, we moms sacrifice and gain new interests for our kids because we love them. Yet the truth is, our son will never love and sacrifice for us to the same degree or extent that we love and sacrifice for him. And that's okay. But he *does* need to learn to give back to his family and support them in their efforts. Otherwise, he'll think the world revolves around him and his interests alone, even though it usually does.

After our two sons regained their faculties, they attended our clogging graduation. They even attended a few clogging performances after that—a *huge* sacrifice. But hey, they needed to learn that their father and I had wooden bleachers reserved for them, too. And they're better men for it today.

A WORD FROM THE WORD:

In humility value others above yourselves, not looking to your own interests but each of you to the interests of others.
PHILIPPIANS 2:3–4 NIV

Think About It. . .

♡ Are you involved in something in which you can include your son? If you volunteer somewhere, take him along (only if age and gender appropriate to do so). Show him what you do. Have him help you with your work. It will give him a greater perspective not only of his mom, but the world around him.

♡ You have accomplishments, too. Have you returned to college? Do you have a new position at work? Tell your son about it. Engage him in your life more as he gets older. He may not show much interest but, through your example, you will be teaching him life lessons he won't forget.

FINAL THOUGHTS:

It goes against a woman's maternal grain to urge her son to show interest in her own interests. Most, if not all of moms, don't even want that. Yet they need to view this matter in another way. Requesting that your son attend an award ceremony in which you are honored or a graduation of any personal accomplishment is not selfish, self-serving, or audacious.

Even when he's at an early age, teach your son to give as well as receive and support as well as be supported. Although girls are more apt to show support, boys aren't wired the same way. So even if he balks, inform your teenager that you expect and would appreciate his support, just as you have given and will continue to give him yours.

• •

75. Mealtime matters, so plan some of those.

• •

Do you ever feel as if you and your family members are darting in different directions? You probably are. Life is hectic. Your son's schedule alone is enough to propel you down the runway in flight from one destination to another: school, practices, after-school activities, the dentist, the eye doctor, church functions, all this in addition to caring for your other children, maintaining their schedules, and juggling your own household and job responsibilities. If you are fortunate, you squeeze in a date with your husband.

That's why it's important to schedule family mealtimes, especially with your adolescent children. With no texting going on at the table or ear buds in place, your son will likely tune into family conversation. At least it's worth a try. What he's less likely to share on the run, he just might share at the dinner table.

Mealtimes invoke interaction, conversation, and enjoyment of one another's company. "Breaking bread" as a family is the perfect setting for reconnecting.

Statistics cite that only one third of families sit down for family meals daily. We dine on the run, usually in our vehicles. Granted, most of us can't rearrange our schedules to eat dinner together daily, but most of us could plan to do so at least two or three times a week.

Whether you break bread with carryout or a home-cooked meal doesn't matter. It's the setting and sitting that count! Begin meals with prayer, then avoid discussing anxiety-inciting issues, otherwise your teenage son, and everyone else, might dread mealtimes. Sitting at the family dinner table shouldn't feel like reclining in a dentist's chair.

Mealtime offers lots of opportunities to share what God is doing in your life and opens spiritual discussions about your faith, void of preachy undertones. And holiday meals present opportunities that reinforce the family with time-honored traditions. Here are a few ideas: At Easter place a plastic egg at each table setting. Type a portion of the Easter story taken from scriptures on a piece of paper and place it inside each egg. Then have every person open their egg and read it aloud in order. End with prayer. Or at Thanksgiving, take turns expressing what each person is most thankful for. Many times, even a tough teenage boy will shed a tear as he expresses thanks.

Teens need to feel secure and connected—an emotion that is most likely lacking when we all scurry in a hurry. Scheduled mealtimes slows us down to a reasonable pace while blessing us with one another's company and promoting genuine interaction.

Author Mary DeTurris Poust wrote: "Our culture tries to convince us on just about every front that more is better. More is a sign of wealth, luxury, power. Gone are the days when meals were moments of connection and conversation; now it's all about consumption and calories."

Christian moms, you can change that in your own homes. Begin this week.

A WORD FROM THE WORD:

They worshiped together at the Temple each day, met in homes for the Lord's Supper, and shared their meals with great joy and generosity.
ACTS 2:46 NLT

Think About It. . .

♡ Don't answer the phone during dinnertime. Voicemail can get it. Remind your teen that electronics at the dinner table are banned, too.

♡ Always begin your meals with prayer.

♡ Solicit help from your kids to help clean up afterward. Clean up can be fun when everyone pitches in. Just prepare for the out-of-control moments that might ensue at the kitchen sink. Some boys just can't resist sprinkling their sibling with the water sprayer.

FINAL THOUGHTS:

Sharing meals together was significant in the early church and recorded throughout the Bible. In the 1950s and before—the days before the explosion of fast food drive-throughs—sitting down to family dinners was a regular, daily practice. Today's culture has changed dramatically. Your time is limited, but you can rearrange your schedule to fit in family meals at least several times a week. You, Mom, hold the key to bringing the family together.

76. When you mess up, fess up.

Christian moms strive to live exemplary lives. But every now and then (cough, cough) our halo slips.

We *try* to curtail our anger and not make inappropriate comments that are less than Christian. For example, in our family, name calling was taboo, and my husband and I were intolerant of rude comments such as "shut up" or "you're stupid."

So you can imagine my teenage sons' exhilaration when they heard me call someone a name for the first time in their adolescent lives. As I drove the boys to some now-forgotten event, another car careened in front of us, forcing me to slam on my brakes and swerve to the side of the road. Instantly, a word popped out of my mouth faster than Jack springs from his box.

"Dipstick!" I barked, as the driver zoomed ahead.

"Did you hear that, Jeff?" son Jimmy yelled from the backseat. "Mom called that guy a dipstick!"

"Wow, Mom, that was great!" Jeff snickered. "You called that guy a name!"

You would have thought I'd uttered my first recognizable word. The jovial twosome were more enthusiastic and excited than if I had just given them permission to take off a week of school to play video games all day, every day.

It was time to tone them down. "I know, guys," I said in my most maternal let's-be-sensible tone. "I shouldn't have said that. I was wrong," I admitted, attempting to counter their gleeful satisfaction and underscore a moral lesson all at the same time. "Name calling is never justified," I stated with conviction.

But no go. They ignored my contrition as their verbal elation continued. "Man, I can't believe it. That was great!" Jimmy said.

"Yeah, Mom. Dipstick!" Jeff added as their comments recounting my blunder continued to bounce back and forth, ad nauseam.

The only thing left to do was wave the white flag. "That's right, I called that guy a dipstick, okay? I mean, do you mind? It happened, so let's just let it go, if that's all right with you?" I spouted.

That only gave them more fodder for the pig sty, and to this day I still hear about that hilarious moment when Mom lost it in unrestrained emotion. All of the sound words of wisdom I had spoken over the years disappeared in the fog of one incident.

"Oh, Mom," my older son finally said, noticing my frustration, "it's okay; you're only human."

It turned out that witnessing my outburst made my sons feel better about themselves because it confirmed to them what I had known all along—I'm less than perfect. Way less. After all, how many times had I thought "idiot!" or "jerk!" but just hadn't vocalized it? Well, let's not go there. I'm still trying to live down "dipstick."

A WORD FROM THE WORD:

Too much talk leads to sin.
Be sensible and keep your mouth shut.
PROVERBS 10:19 NLT

Think About It. . .

- ♡ When you blow it, do you admit your shortcomings? Your son will view that as a positive trait. After all, no one is perfect, and he needs to know, even though you do already.

- ♡ Do you exemplify Christlike qualities in your everyday speech and manner? Strive to allow the Holy Spirit to keep a watch on your mouth and attitudes. Someone is watching.

- ♡ Being human is, well, human. The Bible instructs believers to confess their faults to one another. Sometimes that means you confessing yours to your son.

FINAL THOUGHTS:

A familiar axiom says, "Confession is good for the soul." That's especially true as a parent. When you mess up, fess up. Ask God for forgiveness and allow your son to see how—just like him—you, too, are a work in progress.

77. Find the funny in your home. Encourage humor.

Your teenager is, well, a teenager. He's oozes practical jokes, crazy antics, and just plain foolishness. You, on the other hand, are the serious-minded, no-nonsense voice of reason in the household, a human adhesive that holds it all together. So you roll your eyes as your son slides into the kitchen like a speed skater, swoops up hot biscuits from the cookie sheet, and juggles them in the air blurting out, "Ouch! Ooh! Yikes!"

"Those are for dinner!" you announce as he exits, stuffing biscuits in his mouth like a squirrel storing nuts for the winter. He's running on high-octane energy and you're bottoming out. One thing you know well by now is that boys have tons of pent-up energy. In fact, one mom regularly instructs her teenage son to "go for a run around the block! You need to use some of that energy."

Though it may seem absurd, even if you feel like the walking dead, engage in some mother-son craziness. Trust me, it's therapeutic, especially on those days when you take yourself too seriously—which is like most of the time, right?

Humor gives us a temporary reprieve from daily life with all of its many problems and frustrations. It is, in fact, medicinal. Scientists suggest that laughter reduces stress, lowers blood pressure, boosts the immune system, and actually releases endorphins that diminish physical pain. That alone is reason enough to indulge in a daily dose of laughter.

Dr. Madan Kataria, founder of the International Laughter Club, noted that children laugh three hundred times a day while adults laugh a scant fifteen times. Parents are deluged with bad news and negativity throughout the day, so they only laugh if there is cause to do so. Kids, on the other hand, laugh unconditionally.

Granted, your son can get pretty annoying. But when your emotions are tighter than a fashion model's leggings, it's time to loosen up with some good old-fashioned laughter and fun. Your son can help! Join him in his craziness. Here are a few ways to do that:

♥ **Embark on some banter.** That's right, joke around with your son. Capture his fun nature and run with it.

♥ **Do something unexpected**. Your son knows you well. Surprise him by doing something he'd never expect from you, like singing his favorite band's song. Sure you may not know the words, but hum along and goof around with it. Get him laughing at and with you.

♥ **Take a spin around the kitchen**. Yes, embarrass him (this is only recommended in the confines of your home). Grab his hands and dance around the kitchen when he comes through brimming with unrestrained energy. Give him a run for his money (or lack thereof).

♥ **Watch a funny video or movie together.** A wholesome,

funny movie or sitcom can alter your mood. Laugh aloud together. Sharing a movie is better than sharing a box of candy and less caloric. It serves as a temporary escape.

Did you ever attend a funeral where the eulogy was both heartwarming and humorous? Sharing funny stories about the deceased brings joy and eases pain, at least temporarily. Comedian Bill Cosby once said: "Through humor, you can soften some of the worse blows that life delivers. And once you find laughter, no matter how painful your situation might be, you can survive it."

Laughter's benefits are immediate. They break the tension and lighten heavy loads. The next time the daily grind of responsibilities and problems weigh you down, shake the irritability and engage in humor and laughter. Your son will benefit, as will you. So find the funny in your life!

A WORD FROM THE WORD:

Our mouths were filled with laughter, our tongues
with songs of joy. Then it was said among the nations,
"The Lord has done great things for them."
PSALM 126:2 NIV

Think About It. . .

- 💗 We're way too serious most of the time. So why not make a conscious effort to find some ways to lighten up?

- 💗 What is it about your son that makes you laugh? His silly smile? His dry humor? Glean silly and fun moments from your son's humorous side.

- 💗 When you're in a bad mood, look for the humor in your hullabaloo. A secure person is one who can laugh at herself in the middle of a not-so-funny situation.

Chuck Swindoll said, "People who live above their circumstances usually possess a well-developed sense of humor, because in the final analysis that's what gets them through." Your son needs to learn that lesson, and he will only develop that humor through what he sees and experiences in his home. Are you way too serious? Do you allow your problems to overburden you so much that you halt the flow of laughter in your home? Do yourself and your family a favor by laughing heartily and often.

● ●

78. Investigate his anger; something else is going on.

● ●

Your son is angry. But is his anger just a cover-up for some other emotion? Society stifles the expression of emotions in men. It often starts when he's a small child. "Big boys don't cry" or "Stop whining!" we tell them, hoping to stop what seems like overly dramatic behavior at the time.

So boys choke back tears—and more. As boys grow older, they become experts at deflecting attention away from their true emotions. Instead, they learn to express the only emotion that seems socially acceptable to them, the only one they can comfortably reveal: anger. But hidden beneath that anger is fear, frustration, rejection, hurt, disappointment, vulnerabilities, or sadness.

Some parents actually provoke their sons to anger through repeatedly treating them harshly or unfairly. The scriptures warn parents, saying: "Fathers, do not embitter your children, or they will become discouraged (Colossians 3:21 NIV).

Uncontrolled anger leads to violence in boys, so it's paramount that mothers of sons tune into their kids' rants when they become frequent. What's going on behind the curtain of anger? Is there something happening at school of which you're unaware? Is he afraid? Did something occur in the family that caused him to feel abandoned, hurt, or insecure, or to experience a loss of control?

This is where daily communication with our son helps. When we're involved in his life, we notice changes in his personality more readily. His anger is really a cry for help. And we moms know how to help our sons. Get him to talk about what's really going on deep inside. Make it comfortable for him to express his feelings in a quiet, uninterrupted setting and at a convenient time of the day, not as you're dashing out the door to take him to football practice. It might take days or even weeks to get down to the source of his anger, but don't shrug it off. The longer he harbors anger, the worse it gets.

One mom said that she instantly knew when her son was upset about something. It always manifested in anger. Only after she and her husband sat him down to talk about it would the real emotions erupt, complete with belly sobs. Rather than stifling those expressions, they allowed their son to come to terms with his feelings and encouraged him to release them in the loving environment of their home.

Teach your son there is a time for anger. Consider Jesus' display of anger when the money changers defiled the temple. Anger, when used correctly, can become a motivator to change circumstances. Our objective as moms is to help our sons learn how to manage their anger so it doesn't run rampant and cause Satan to gain a foothold in their lives.

If they learn early to allow the Holy Spirit to search their hearts and help them with what's really bothering them, they are on the pathway to success spiritually and emotionally. Dr. Harriet Lerner said, "Anger is a signal and one worth listening to." Listen to your son's anger, Mom. He may be trying to tell you something.

A WORD FROM THE WORD:

Do not provoke your children to anger by the way you treat them. Rather, bring them up with the discipline and instruction that comes from the Lord.
EPHESIANS 6:4 NLT

Think About It. . .

♡ Everyone gets angry. But does your son exhibit anger more than usual? If so, he might be harboring deeper issues to address. Talk to him and get professional help if necessary.

♡ Let him vent with respect. In other words, allow him to express his anger within acceptable limits—no name calling or displays of disrespect to his siblings or you and other people in authority.

♡ Sometimes anger is not only understandable, it's necessary. If he's the object of bullying and approaching authorities would embarrass him, then teach him how to stand up for himself and exhibit self-confidence and respect. If he doesn't respect himself, others won't either. Instruct him how to handle these situations without becoming a bully himself.

♡ Ask your son these questions: "Why do you think you get so angry when. . . ?" "What's really bothering you? You can tell me; I'm here to listen." Then do it. Listen. Give your son the opportunity to unload his thoughts without judgment or criticism. Then love him back to a place of security.

FINAL THOUGHTS:

Anger is a natural emotion. The key is to instruct your son how to control it. Often, even he is unaware of the underlying reasons. It's up to you to help him unmask those hidden emotions, to get to the core of what's really bothering him.

Perhaps remind your son that the apostle Paul was impulsive and hotheaded, vacillating from one extreme to another. But after his conversion, Christ transformed him to channel his weaknesses into strengths. He was one of the most courageous and bold champions of the gospel.

Pray together for and with your son. Anger should not control him; rather, he will learn to control his anger with God's help and your loving support.

79. Accept the five-second rule. It makes perfect sense to your son and probably to his dad.

Your son drops a piece of candy on the floor, swiftly scoops it up hoping you didn't see him, and pops it into his mouth. You glare his way, and he volleys a snappy response: "It was only there a few seconds!"

To my surprise and consternation, my dear, tidy, clean-conscious husband initiated what was touted as "the five-second rule" in our household, which was comprised of two boys, one husband, and me, the lone female. This seemingly idiotic rule held that whatever food fell to the floor and was retrieved in five seconds was deemed sanitary and germ-free, suitable for swallowing. Our sons jumped on board with this precept faster than a hobo ascends a boxcar. From that moment on, the five-second rule was enforced despite my grumblings and objections. Three males against one female creates poor odds.

What makes perfect sense to males is ridiculous to females and vice versa. Males are sticklers for details and experts at shortcuts riddled with logic. If you're inundated with males in your home, you know exactly what that means.

"Why make the bed?" your husband inquires. "We'll be sleeping in it again tonight."

Meanwhile, you defend global domesticity, replying, "If you buy that theory, then why do anything? Why wash your car or clean the garage? Why shave, brush your teeth, or take a shower? You'll just have to do it again."

Regardless, you've lost the battle on the five-second rule, a precept that is firmly sealed within their male minds. And nothing deters them—not even your consistent glare of disapproval. So we moms must pick our battles, because it's clear we'll lose this one anyway. And if you consider how your male children eat apart from your presence, five seconds on the floor is clean compared to them eating anything and everything with dirty, grimy hands that have been who-knows-where.

Let's face it. Eating food that dropped to the floor is the least of your worries. Your son's soul—the choices he makes, the values he embraces, and the life he lives for Christ—are issues worth fighting for. So surrender to the five-second rule. It's bound to last awhile regardless.

Think About It. . .

♡ What you question, your son accepts with little or no thought. That's part of his makeup. Priorities differ from the male's point of view. The sooner females learn that about males, the easier life becomes.

♡ Enforce the rules that matter. Of course, cleanliness and good hygiene are important. (See Tip 59.) But allowing yourself to get bent out of shape for little reason overtaxes you and all the men in the house.

FINAL THOUGHTS:

Your son's reasoning is often illogical and downright annoying. This is where the male versus female reasoning butts heads like two warring billy goats. So ask yourself, "Is this really worth the battle?" If not, just roll your eyes and walk on.

80. Embrace his masculinity and provide positive male role models.

Did you notice how the media and our culture slowly weaken a male's self-perception? The general media's stereotypical idea of men is that they are the bane of our society and the source of all our problems. (Okay, maybe they are in some cases, but let's be fair.)

Movies and sitcoms portray males as bumbling, sex-driven idiots while females are lauded as strong, independent individuals who are able to grind men into dust physically and emotionally. Just turn on a television program: Women dominate men from the police department to the loading docks.

Women in particular should know how that type of negative typecasting feels. So why would we turn the table and treat our sons like lower-class citizens? Don't allow society to emasculate your son. Teach him that, yes, men and women are equal, but their roles are totally different. God created us that way.

That's not to say that we shouldn't expect him to show compassion, kindness, thoughtfulness, and expressions of caring and love. On the contrary, his best role model is God Himself. The Lord is all-powerful, yet He is also all-loving, compassionate, and overwhelmingly sensitive to the needs of others.

Males are more emotionally grounded than we are. They are less likely to flitter in all directions like a butterfly on steroids. By observing his dad and other positive male role models, your son learns how to tackle and solve problems with wisdom and discretion and how to master manhood with honor, sensitivity, integrity, and strength.

Should a positive male role model be absent, teach your son these attributes as you would teach him anything else. Seek out sources of assistance through your church or your son's school. If his father is unavailable, perhaps his grandfather or another close family member will step in and help direct him from a man's point of view.

Be open and show love, respect, and admiration for your son's father. (See Tip 27.) Frequent displays of genuine affection between you and your spouse reinforce your son's perception of a godly marriage and home life. How you and your husband treat one another is how your son will treat his future wife.

Author and evangelist Josh McDowell wrote: "We do not develop habits of genuine love automatically. We learn by watching effective role models—most specifically by observing how our parents express love for each other day in and day out."

If you desire your son to mature and one day enter into a committed relationship; if you want him to become a man of courage and strength, yet caring and loving enough to consider the feelings of others; if you pray that he will exemplify characteristics like honor, respect, integrity, honesty, and courage, then help him embrace his masculinity now. Let him know that becoming a man isn't growing facial hair—it's embodying strong godly characteristics!

A WORD FROM THE WORD:

But you, man of God, flee from all this, and pursue righteousness, godliness, faith, love, endurance and gentleness.
1 TIMOTHY 6:11 NIV

Think About It. . .

♡ Your son wants to embrace his masculinity, but everywhere he turns he's getting dumped on. Pick up God's Word to show him who real men are. Turn to some of the champions in the Bible or to everyday modern examples of strong, honorable, men of God he can emulate.

♡ The Lord desires for your son to become a godly man, strong yet gentle. Exhibiting love, understanding, and compassion isn't wimpy; it's honorable. Teach your son that living the Christian life isn't for wimps. It takes a strong, committed man to follow Jesus.

♡ Do you respect your son's differences? Embrace his masculine traits as you do your husband's.

♡ Especially as your son matures, avoid humiliating or shaming him in public (or at home for that matter).

FINAL THOUGHTS:

While society vilifies men, women have the opportunity to adjust that portrayal in their own homes. Your son is the future minister, CEO, physician, or hard-working laborer. He is also tomorrow's dad, husband, and leader. In a world that degrades him daily, encourage him. Show how much you respect his father and respect your son's masculinity. Help him to unmask the essentials that make a boy a *real* man.

81. When your son suffers from repeated memory loss, forget to make his dinner.

As moms, we try to make reasonable requests. "Okay, listen up everyone. After you shower, wipe down the tile." That's not unreasonable, is it? This simple gesture saves you time so that you can engage in other activities besides scrubbing, disinfecting, and wiping.

Maybe you made a request similar to this one, and two of your teenage boys actually adhered for two days—one day for each son. After that, it became too much for their bulging muscles to handle. That's when the excuses flowed faster than the time it takes to evacuate the kitchen after mealtime.

"But I wasn't the *last* one to shower," one son protests. Or "I'm running late. I'll do it later, Mom." You've heard that before. Later, as in sometime-long-after-Mom's-buffed-the-tile-squeaky-clean-and-it-doesn't-need-wiping-down-anymore later. Somehow simple requests are the hardest for teenage boys to follow.

Sudden memory loss occurs whenever you ask him to dispose of the garbage (both in the kitchen and under his bed), feed the dog, pick up his dirty clothes, or stack the dishes in the dishwasher instead of piling them, dripping with food scraps, inside the sink.

"Oops, sorry, I forgot" is a common phrase that is supposed to trigger immediate clemency from you. Yet this same boy has a photographic memory to recite the intricacies of his video games and his personal Gamerscores, his favorite baseball players' individual batting averages, or what recreational activities he has planned three weeks from Saturday.

Admittedly, we all are guilty of the same shortcoming. God has a few requests, too: Read the Bible, pray, obey, love one another. Those aren't unreasonable requests, yet we, too, are like our teenage sons when it comes to following through. Have you ever thought, *I'm so busy right now; I'll read my Bible later,* or prayed, "Sorry, Lord, I forgot," hoping to invoke God's instant approval?

Yet we remember when our favorite television program runs, what hours the mall is open, or what day we have off work. Only when problems arise or life gets rocky do we remember the importance of spending time doing what the Lord asks of us. The bottom line for all of us, including our forgetful sons, is that our good intentions are meaningless without corresponding actions.

So after you wipe down the shower tile (again), turn the tables to initiate some incentive. Try the memory-loss excuse; namely, be apologetic yet insincere. When your teenage son returns home and scans the stovetop for signs of dinner, tell him, "Oops, sorry, honey, I forgot."

Then prepare for a response something like this: "You forgot to make dinner."

"Yep, I just didn't have enough time."

"Well, then when do we eat, Mom?"

"Later, sweetie. Much, much later."

Amazingly, you might just find that he'll soon stop using the memory-loss excuse the next time you ask him to follow through with a simple request.

A WORD FROM THE WORD:

"Watch and pray. . . The spirit is willing, but the flesh is weak."
MATTHEW 26:41 NIV

Think About It. . .

♡ Your son doesn't deliberately intend to ignore your requests. He's just so tied up in his own thoughts and life that your solicitations aren't high on his agenda. So it takes a little feather ruffling to get your point across. Try it.

💙 Simple summons are complex orders to a teenage boy. Make your requests clear and concise with a time frame involved, such as: "Take out the trash every day directly after dinner. That's your job and your responsibility." If he fails, remind him once more and add corresponding consequences, if you haven't done so already. He'll get the message when his cell phone, game, or computer time is put on hold.

FINAL THOUGHTS:

Teenage boys are wonderful, sweet, and mindless all at the same time. Establish chores for him to do or errands to run if he is old enough to drive. Let him know what you expect and, if he repeatedly forgets to follow through, give him a few mom-creative incentives!

82. Discuss the dangers of peer pressure.

"Everybody does it," your son responds after you tell him he can't do something his friends are doing. You volley a snappy response: "If your friends jump off a cliff, will you follow them?"

The age-old issue of peer pressure has plagued parents from the beginning of time. The temptation to follow his contemporaries coerces the best, most well-behaved kids to cross boundaries in an attempt to become one of the guys.

One mom described her frustration. She raised her son with godly values and standards. For the most part, he breezed through his high school years without incident. But after he left home for college, he unraveled like a spool of runaway thread. At first, he complained about the behavior he witnessed in his dormitory. He attended a Christian college, so the mom was mortified to hear what went on: drinking, sex, even homosexual activity. During her son's sophomore year, she noticed changes in him. Gradually, the more he interacted with his peers, the further the years of teaching and raising her son in the ways of the Lord went down the tube.

Why is peer pressure so powerful? Because your son, like you, desires acceptance from his peers. Think about it: Have you ever, for fear of making waves or gaining enemies, kept silent while a crowd of ladies gossiped? That's peer pressure. Did you ever go along with someone rather than take a stand because you wanted that person to like you? Peer pressure. What about the desire to fit in? That emotion isn't reserved for teenagers. Adults, too, seek acceptance from their coworkers, employers, church groups, or organizations.

So it is with your growing son. He's trying to find his place in this world and fit in. He's faced with challenging decisions daily. "Come on, try one cigarette," a friend suggests. "One won't hurt." Or, "Hey, I'm going to a party. Everybody will be there. Wanna come?" Or maybe his friends post questionable things on social media outlets. Your son not only seeks peer approval but avoids acting like the odd-man-out to avert ridicule or bullying. That's why peer pressure is so dangerous and potent.

So what can a mother do? If your son senses parental love and acceptance and exhibits positive self-esteem, you've won half the battle. Writer Walt Mueller wisely noted: "No matter what they look like or how they act, all teenagers are yearning for adult love and acceptance. Kids who give in easily to peer pressure and go wrong are typically kids who lack the input, love, and acceptance of a significant adult in their lives."

Talk to him about the dangers and adverse consequences of succumbing to peer pressure and how it can affect his life negatively. Advise him that he doesn't have to respond to questionable things his friends post on the Internet. Warn him about the long-standing consequences that reckless and inappropriate social-media behavior has. Help him to think through some possible scenarios before they actually happen. Ask him questions like, "If someone offers you alcohol, drugs, or cigarettes, what will you tell them? How will you handle it? If a girl pressures you to have sex, what will you do?" Then offer him some suggestions on how to handle the hounding. Remind him that preventing others to strong-arm him is a sign of strength, power, and maturity. Kids will respect him for his solid convictions, and he might just influence other boys to follow his lead.

Your son faces more challenges today than you did when you

were his age. He needs your support and guidance. Know who his friends are and what they are allowed to do. If "everyone is doing it," he needs to find friends who aren't.

Think About It. . .

♡ "You are what you eat" says one common axiom. Likewise, a person becomes like the people with whom he associates. Encourage your son to choose his friends wisely. Just because someone is popular doesn't make him good company to keep.

♡ One of anything isn't just one; it is an opening for more of the same. Explain that to your son when his peers tell him that just one drink, cigarette, or drug won't hurt. It will. Big time.

♡ Some friends might think that shoplifting is fun and exciting. Inform your son that these kinds of adventurous activities are against the law, and there's nothing fun or funny about a jail cell or criminal record.

♡ Peer pressure is just that: pressure. Teach your son that God gives us a free will to choose good or evil. Anyone or anything that dictates, dominates, controls, or pressures us isn't from God but Satan.

FINAL THOUGHTS:

Don't you wish you could just wave a wand and banish all of the exterior pressures your son faces? Unfortunately, you can't. He has to learn how to say "no" and take a stand on his own. He must learn to form his own set of convictions and stick to them. He *will* cave in to peer pressure, just like we all have at one time or another. But he'll learn, just as you did, with a little assistance and guidance and a whole lot of prayer.

83. Be his greatest fan, best critic, and biggest supporter; it's part of your job description.

No one cheers louder for your son than you do. *Well, maybe his dad in a much deeper and louder voice.* No one understands him better or thinks of him more. You are the one who cradled him as a baby and nurtured him as he grew. You tended to his boo-boos great and small. Whenever he was sick, you had one ear open all night long while he slept, ready to jump to his bedside the moment he cried or called your name. Now you forfeit sleep and watch the clock, waiting for him to return home from an evening date or a group outing.

You know his faults and understand his weaknesses but love him in spite of them all. His smallest accomplishments were and still are giant feats to you, worthy of bragging about, even though you try to withhold your maternal pride. You defend him, protect him, and sacrifice for him. He's your boy and that will never change.

You are also notorious for doling constructive criticism when needed. Who else will tell him that his pants are too baggy or his hair is too long? Who will instruct him to straighten up and fly right? Regardless, you maintain your status as your son's biggest supporter and truest friend. You see his potential to make first string on his school's basketball team, even though he can't dribble the ball. You believe in him, while others scratch their heads in wonder. You have plans for him—big ones. Even if he has limited talent, you believe he can become whatever he chooses and support him in his efforts. You're not naïve, just hopeful. You're a boundless encourager and prayer warrior.

The love between a mother and son is precious, priceless, and secure. Someone once wisely noted: "There never has been, nor will there ever be, anything quite so special as the love between a mother and a son." A mom's heart is intertwined with her son's heart indefinitely.

Only one other person loves your son more than you do: Jesus. In fact, your love for him emulates God's love for each of us. It is unconditional and lasting. Washington Irving put it this way: "A mother is the truest friend we have when trials, heavy and sudden, fall upon us; when adversity takes the place of prosperity; when friends who rejoice with us in our sunshine, desert us when troubles thicken around us, still will she cling to us, and endeavor by her kind precepts and counsels to dissipate the clouds of darkness, and cause peace to return to our hearts."

Isn't that how God loves us? The below scripture describes God's unconditional love. In fact, the definition of God *is* love. Somehow He seals His love in our hearts and minds for our son. Although boys drive us crazy with their antics and aggravate us with their all-boy ways, they hold our hearts.

Your son may not express it for years to come—or possibly not at all—but you are his best cheerleader (despite what the little girl in the short skirt expresses at his basketball games). Root him on! Let him know that if and when everyone else falls to the wayside, you'll still stand with him. So keep supporting your boy, Mom. It's part of your job description.

A WORD FROM THE WORD:

Love is patient and kind. Love is not jealous or boastful or proud or rude. It does not demand its own way. It is not irritable, and it keeps no record of being wronged. It does not rejoice about injustice but rejoices whenever the truth wins out. Love never gives up, never loses faith, is always hopeful, and endures through every circumstance.

1 CORINTHIANS 13:4–7 NLT

Think About It. . .

♡ Does your son know how much you care? If you're not sure, remind him today.

♡ Consider the quote by Connie Grigsby and Kent Julian: "Do we want our teens to talk to us? Then nothing is more important than the strength of our own integrity, faith, and character. If our teens trust and respect us and feel secure in our unconditional love they will talk to us."

♡ The scriptures say that "love covers a multitude of sins" (1 Peter 4:8 NLT). You might not like everything your son does, but you love him in spite of it.

FINAL THOUGHTS:

Love is a word used loosely and way too often. Although there are different interpretations of the word *love*, God's love is the only one that is pure, lasting, and unconditional. It's the kind your heavenly Father has for you, the kind you want to have for your son.

• •

84. After your son becomes a driving expert, expect lots of advice.

• •

So your son finally got his much-coveted drivers' license. And you discover that his two weeks behind the wheel has made him a driving expert. How do you know that? Because your sixteen-year-old son tells you everything you're doing wrong when you take the driver's seat. Each driving maneuver, subject to his scrutiny, must be done with precision and accuracy. If not, expect to hear about it.

Susan told the story of how, having undergone numerous encounters listening to her son issue driving instructions, she had finally had enough. "Look, Jake," she said firmly, "need I remind you that I have been driving for twenty-five long years now? I think I know a bit more about driving than you do!"

"Yeah, Mom, I know," Jake responded, "but I'm just telling you what the book says."

The book? What book? Susan asked herself. *Since when does a* veteran at the wheel need to peruse a driver's manual? After twenty-five years, who needs instructions anymore?

In a moment of self-examination, Susan noticed her pride swelling like a soaked disposable diaper. As if on cue, this scripture came to mind: "When pride comes, then comes disgrace, but with humility comes wisdom" (Proverbs 11:2 NIV). The verse reminded her that years of routinely doing something a certain way doesn't necessarily mean it's done correctly, a point brought home by Susan's teenage teacher.

Have you ever realized that your son actually has the capacity to teach you a few things? Although too much instruction is annoying and even disrespectful at times, a mom should, at the very least, listen to her son's advice, albeit unsolicited. After all, we need instruction manuals to help us put together a book shelf, program a DVR, use a new appliance, work a smart phone, and, yes, even bone up on driving rules and regulations.

The Bible is our ultimate source of truth and instruction. It holds the monopoly on truth void of worldly values, newest trends, or even years of prior experience. In fact, God's Word is the original drivers' manual of life. It teaches us that pride is the attitude that will stunt our spiritual and emotional growth no matter how seasoned a "driver" we think we are!

A wise mom opens her heart and mind to her growing son's opinions, although you hold the last word. Besides, there's always room for more instruction. But don't take my word for it. I'm just telling you what the Book says!

A WORD FROM THE WORD:

Whoever gives heed to instructions prospers.
PROVERBS 16:20 NIV

Think About It. . .

♡ Are you irritated whenever your son voices his strong opinions? Remember he's growing up, forming his own thoughts and ideas. Gently guide him through God's Word, then pray for him and leave the rest to God.

♡ Moms worry about their sons behind the wheel. Boys are notorious for driving too fast with music blaring. Give your son a few instructions of your own, and follow up on him. No texting and driving. Is he consistently using his seatbelt? Does he abide by the speed limit? Stay on top of such matters.

FINAL THOUGHTS:

Moms are so used to issuing directives and enforcing rules that they often fail to notice their own flaws and shortcomings. You'll never stop learning. Sometimes it's just hard taking advice from a teenage boy!

85. He's your best ally; the older he gets, the more he defends you.

One thirty-six-year-old mom was an avid jogger. In good physical shape, she appeared younger than her chronological age. As she ran her usual jogging route one summer afternoon, a teenage boy made a suggestive comment. Upset, the mom stopped dead in her tracks, turned around, and chastised the boy for his impropriety. Still seething, she finished her run and entered the house in a huff. Her teenage son overheard his mom tell his dad what had just happened.

Like an arrow released from the bow, her son darted from the house in search of the kid who had made the inappropriate comment to his mom. Despite her insistence and his father's command to return home, the angered son was on a mission. Someone stepped out of line with his mom and he wasn't about to let it go.

Even at a young age your son will defend you. Should someone say something unkind or angry, your boy will retaliate, usually with a verbal scolding. Say what you want about him, but don't attack his mommy!

Moms protect their young at any cost; likewise, boys protect their mother's name like none other. To bash a boy's mom is to slice the artery of his life. Even the most timid individual roars in anger if his mom is defamed in any way.

Just as a husband protects and cherishes his wife and family, a son honors and defends his mom or sister. Besides your husband, your son is your greatest ally and strongest defender. Honoré de Balzac asked, "Is there any instinct more deeply implanted in the heart of man than the pride of protection, a protection which is constantly exerted for a fragile and defenseless creature?" Although some ladies might take exception to the description "fragile and defenseless," you get the point.

God Himself is our protector and defender. He watches over us and leads us to safety. He guides us with a loving heart and keen eye; He stands in at our defense against the enemy of our souls. Our Father protects us under the shadow of His mighty, outstretched arms. What a wonderful place to reside!

And although he may not consciously know it and might not readily show it, your son is protective of you, too. He'll defend you to his friends and protect you against all enemies. God made him that way.

A WORD FROM THE WORD:

It [love] always protects, always trusts,
always hopes, always perseveres.
1 CORINTHIANS 13:7 NIV

Think About It. . .

♡ Instruct your son to temper his anger when he gets too protective of you or family members.

♡ Defending others is a godly attribute only when tempered with self-control.

♡ Your son is loyal, and that is a noble characteristic. Loyalty wins wars, builds homes, forgives transgressions, and exhibits spiritual strength. Remind your son that, although you appreciate and value his loyalty, retaliation is never the answer.

FINAL THOUGHTS:

Your son's need to protect you stems from his love for you and your family. The older he becomes, the more aware he is of derogatory remarks aimed toward you, or disrespectful attitudes or actions coming from others. Boys are protectors but they are also given to aggressive retaliation. Teach your son how to control his anger should he run to your defense.

• •

86. It doesn't take a village to raise a boy; it takes faith and a metropolitan city.

• •

Whether or not you realize it, everything you do is done in faith. You go to sleep at night, confident of morning. You eat expecting nourishment, and you breathe in air that you can't see. It takes faith to allow your teenage son behind the wheel of your car, and faith to believe that there is life beyond the bassinet! In faith, a desperate mom cries out to God for her prodigal son or intercedes for her sick child.

Your son notices your faith. He watches and listens to his parents when you think he's tucked away somewhere out of eyesight or earshot. Boys have eagle eyes and elephant ears. They absorb everything around them, especially the words and actions of their elders.

Parents who build their house on the rock of Jesus Christ stand tall during the worst of adversities. Is your home built on the Rock? How do we create this godly infrastructure anyway? Is faith enough?

Moms who build their homes based on godly principles recorded in God's Word and who prioritize matters like prayer, daily devotions, and church attendance set the groundwork on which everything else stands.

Extended family who assist you in the faith-building process are a double blessing. A church family and pastor who cares about your kids are priceless. Both blood and spiritual relatives, eager to add faith to your son's life, are a metropolitan city of support, encouragement, patience, and faith at work.

But you and his dad are the biggest influences in your son's life, and no one can replace you. Is Christ at the center of your life? Your home? If He is, your son will sense the presence of the Holy Spirit in and through you. Roger J. Squire said, "It ought to be as impossible to forget that there is a Christian in the house as it is to forget that there is a ten-year-old boy in it."

Preach a little, but live your faith a lot. Ultimately, your son will choose whether or not to follow your example to accept Jesus. Author Ron Hutchcraft wrote: "Teenagers are not interested in hearing about religion, denomination, or lifestyle issues. It is the person of Jesus that will interest a modern young person, not the system of Christianity."

If you are more church or religion-oriented than Christ-oriented, your son will catch that and it won't impress him much, especially as he matures and formulates ideas of his own. Through your prayer and example, you can trust that your son will accept forgiveness through Jesus Christ if he hasn't already. If he has already asked Christ into his heart, your prayers and examples of faith in action will keep him in the center of God's will for his life.

Our adolescent sons want the real deal. They look for substance, meaning, and authentic examples of faith. Minister and author Chuck Swindoll said it bluntly: "You want to mess up the minds of your children? Here's how—guaranteed! Rear them in a legalistic, tight context of external religion, where performance is more important than reality. Fake your faith. Sneak around and pretend your spirituality. Train your children to do the same. Embrace a long list of do's and don'ts publicly but hypocritically practice them privately. . . yet never own up to the fact that it's hypocrisy. Act one way but live another. And you can count on it—emotional and spiritual damage will occur."

Martin Luther's wife, Katharina Von Bora, said these final words before she passed into eternity: "I will stick to Christ as a burr to a topcoat!" As you demonstrate your faith in Christ, you substantiate that He is your foundation, your topcoat. And as you cleave to Him like a burr and live for God—not just talk about Him—your son will cleave to Christ, too.

Think About It. . .

♡ Faith is seeing your son go astray, yet believing God is
bigger than your son's rebellion. Faith sees him as he will
be, not as he is.

♡ Does your firm foundation have some cracks in it? Or maybe
you just feel the foundation shake every now and then. Take
it to God; He's the master builder and repairer.

♡ Don't force your faith; live it. Faith is personal and real.

♡ Our faith isn't based on current trends but on the scriptures.
Read them often and aloud. Stand on them.

FINAL THOUGHTS:

You might think you have little faith, but that's all you need. The
mustard seed is miniature in size but mighty in power. Use the faith
you have and watch it grow! Then watch your son's faith emerge, too.

• •

87. Acquaint your son with the lost art of chivalry.

• •

Does your husband hold the door open for you? Does he help you
with your coat or allow you to order first at a restaurant? If so, he's
teaching your son the art of chivalry without even knowing it. Many
men don't realize how their sons mirror their actions, attitudes, and
words. But this book isn't directed toward them. It's all about you and

your son. If you are a single mom or don't have a chivalrous husband, you can still raise a gentleman.

Teach your son that one of his God-ordained roles is to love, protect, and cherish women. Insist that your son show you and all women respect. That includes his annoying sister as well! Boys need to learn to hold girls in high regard. So hitting his sister is out. In the Bible, young Timothy wrote: "Treat older women as you would your mother, and treat younger women with all purity as you would your own sisters" (1 Timothy 5:2).

A teenage boy needs to comprehend how important it is to respect girls. As his body changes, his mind focuses on the sexual nature associated with girls. This is the time to help him understand and embrace godly principles regarding the opposite sex. Explain that a girl isn't an object for his personal use; rather, she is one of God's beautiful creations, designed to fulfill God's plan for his life. Instruct him to honor and cherish all women as God intended.

With that in mind, teach your son simple gentlemanly gestures like carrying heavy items for a girl or meeting his date's parents. Instruct him what is appropriate or inappropriate speech and behavior around girls and women. Talk to him about a girl's sensitive nature so that he doesn't say unkind things in jest, leaving her wounded and hurt. Talk to him about the characteristics girls admire in a boy. Your son is clueless about girls, and you are the main person in his life who can fill him in accurately. At the same time, his dad's advice is priceless. He can share things with your teenage son from a godly man's perspective.

In the name of equality with men, some women bristle at a man opening her door or allowing her to take his seat on a crowded bus. How tragic! Chivalry should be applauded in men, not discouraged.

I appreciate my gentlemanly husband. When he holds a door open, carries my groceries—better yet, when he *does* the grocery shopping for me—or insists on picking up heavy packages, I feel loved and honored as a woman. His thoughtfulness spares me from trudging through a snowy, slushy parking lot as he insists I wait for him at the door while he gets the car. He's considerate enough to watch when my gas tank nears empty so he can fill it for me. He has a keen sense of chivalry not just for me, but for all women.

I like the quote that reads: "If you're not raising your boys to respect women, they will never become men." Teach your son that real men are real gentlemen with a healthy, genuine respect for women.

Donna Lynn Hope defined the waning art of chivalry this way: "Chivalry: It's the little boy that kisses my hand, the young man who holds the door open for me, and the old man who tips his hat to me. None of it is a reflection of me, but a reflection of them."

Your son needs to know that how he treats a girl or woman is a reflection on him, his values, and his character. Girls are attracted to guys who treat them well. And a gentleman is a wonderful asset in any marriage.

The waning art of chivalry is due for a comeback in a big way. Your son just might be one of many males who will play a part in promoting this courteous and virtuous behavior in the next generation of males. It all begins now, with you. Instruct your son to show respect and care for women through attentive, considerate gestures and gentlemanly actions. Chivalry need not end up becoming a lost art but a hidden treasure about to be unearthed.

A WORD FROM THE WORD:

She must be well respected by everyone because of the good she has done. Has she brought up her children well?
1 TIMOTHY 5:10 NLT

Think About It. . .

♡ God's Word admonishes male believers to respect and honor women despite their age, race, or status. The more your son practices acts of courtesy toward women, the more he will perform such acts.

♡ Does your son treat you with dignity? Allow him to hold open doors for you and exhibit gentleman-like behavior early. A six-feet-five son might tower over his mom's five-feet-three frame, but he will always know who is in charge when he respects her.

♡ What you and your husband teach him now about women

will carry throughout his lifetime. Raise a gentleman, and his future spouse will thank you.

💔 Does your son respect women in general? Or is he demeaning and rude? What are your personal expectations of how your son treats the opposite sex?

FINAL THOUGHTS:

Gallantry, courtesy, and honor are noble qualities a knight in shining armor should wear like a badge of courage and strength to defend and protect the weak and innocent. This is where *chivalry* derived its meaning. The demonstration of these characteristics is needed and relevant in today's world, now more than ever. The code of chivalry is a handbook of good conduct and glowing gallantry. Remember, every gentleman is a man, but not every man is a gentleman.

• •

88. Is your son leaving for college or a trade school? Grab a tissue now, and again when he returns home.

• •

High school graduation is a bittersweet time for moms and sons. When my firstborn, Jimmy, graduated from high school, I was traumatized. Anticipating his departure for college was more painful than a tooth extraction.

On a warm Sunday morning our minister summoned the graduates and their parents to the front of the church. I grabbed a wad of tissues before ascending to the platform, knowing I'd need them. After the pastor distributed token gifts, prayed for the graduates, and expressed congratulations, we filed back to our pews.

Attempting to withhold my sobs, I clutched the tissues, pressing them against my quivering lips. But just before I sat down, an elderly gray-haired lady reached out to grab my sleeve. "Don't worry," she whispered with a sheepish grin, "he'll be back."

Her words, like my offspring, returned to haunt me, causing me to wonder if my emotional brouhaha was simply a case of temporary insanity. Although my sons are mature, responsible adults, now with families of their own, in their early twenties they both returned to the roost for a period of time.

Having spoken with other former melodramatic mothers, I have concluded that today's adult chicks cling to the nest with both claws. I even met such offspring. His name was Bill—a bright, responsible, twenty-five-year-old man who sat next to me on a flight home to Chicago. He was an accounting major, employed by a big firm.

"So do you live close to your parents?" I asked, having talked with him for a while.

He grinned. "Yeah, I live *real* close. I live with them."

Now I realize that I am addressing some mourning moms who, like I once did, weep at the thought of their firstborn's flight. But don't worry. He'll be back, because experience tells me that the elderly gray-haired lady spoke the truth.

Trust me on this. No matter how much you love your sons, one day the pitter patter of sizes 11 and 13 feet won't nudge you to peruse *Parents Magazine* anymore. You might even find yourselves devising an insidious plan of escape. "When they finally leave, let's sell the house, move to another state, and forget to leave a forwarding address," you whisper to hubby.

But in all probability, some day you'll be tripping over your adult son's shoes while removing his damp, mildewed laundry from the washing machine. And just like me you'll wipe your tears for a much different reason, wondering if the next time you see that wise gray-haired lady, she'll have better news.

A WORD FROM THE WORD:

Be happy with those who are happy,
and weep with those who weep.
ROMANS 12:15 NLT

Think About It. . .

♡ Unprepared emotionally for your son's departure? It's tough.

You try to prepare him and yourself for the day he leaves home, but letting go isn't something that comes naturally to moms. Give yourself, and him, time to adjust. You both will.

♡ Often, attending local college or trade school is a good start to the "letting go" process. If your son isn't ready to embark on campus life away from home, offer alternatives.

♡ College and trade-school life is scary. Do what you can beforehand to make the transition easier for your son. Visit the school, talk to students and faculty, and familiarize your son and yourselves with his new surroundings long before he leaves.

♡ If you son opts not to go to college or a trade school but begins working right away, he may stay at home longer than you think. Take advantage of these moments for one day soon, he will be heading out that door.

FINAL THOUGHTS:

Mothers hold, mold, and then finally let go. Letting go is the hardest part! After all, you have nurtured, instructed, guided, molded, protected, and loved your son for eighteen long years. Now you are supposed to just let him loose? Hopefully, you have been letting go gradually for years prior to this time of his life. Nevertheless, this separation is yet another integral part of his development and growth. So as you navigate this difficult transition, hang in there. And remember that one day, you might just tear up when he moves back home.

• •

89. Tolerate him until college break ends.

• •

You have survived sending your son off to college or trade school to settle into life without your daily presence. At first you struggled, but now you enjoy the parental perks of this stage in his life and yours. For one, his room stays clean, at least until he comes home for holidays and school breaks. But he's different now. Way different. He's been on his own for a few months, wallowing in his dirt-laden dormitory complete with smelly socks, half-empty soda cans, and pizza boxes that contain dried, moldy chunks of crust.

So he comes home for the holidays and his once-clean room turns into a junkyard. Cautiously you tread on his turf. You wonder how a quarter inch of dust covers every conceivable place in such a narrow window of time. You run your finger across his dresser and ask, "What's this?"

"Dust," he answers, without missing a strum on his guitar.

An empty milk glass with Oreo cookie crumbs permanently embedded on the bottom sits on his nightstand. Clothes—you're unable to decipher if they're clean or dirty, but you suspect the latter—are scattered across the room like a flea market in progress. CDs, loose change, magazines, and ticket stubs cover all surfaces. "It's easier to find them that way," he explains.

"How can you live like this?" you blurt out.

"What?" he answers with a searching gaze.

You realize you're fighting a losing battle; yet this, after all, is still your house. "Son, I want this pigsty cleaned, and I want it cleaned now!" you order as you stomp away.

Ten minutes later you are making a valiant effort to curb your frustration. Meanwhile, you notice that your son isn't bothered much, which makes you even angrier. He even has the audacity to hum while he nonchalantly wanders around his room.

Whenever we challenge our sons, we hope to make an impact of some sort—to arouse attention, promote concern, initiate change. Unfortunately, what we discover instead is that what upsets us is of little or no concern to them. Nevertheless, we still attempt to persuade our out-of-the-nest son to experience the same degree of convictions that we have.

The lesson here is that no matter what you've instilled in your son throughout his growing up years, after he ventures outside the home he begins to form his own lifestyle and opinions. Although in all probability, he already formed his opinions long before he left home. The difference now is that he is free to live his lifestyle of choice. *And all the mothers collectively sigh, "Ugh!"*

So whenever you tread on his turf, brace yourself for a few surprises. Inevitably, the way he lives is disproportionate to the way you live. The reality is, after your son leaves your home the major portion of your parenting is already completed, and it is time for you to slack off and allow him to make his own choices.

When he returns home from school, you can expect to see changes. Some good, some not to your liking. Regardless, continue to love him unconditionally, believing that the Lord is working in his life just as He has and does in yours. Meanwhile, just hold out long enough for him to return to school after the holiday break. Then you can happily get back to normal.

A WORD FROM THE WORD:

"Do not be afraid, for I am with you; I will bring your children from the east and gather you from the west."
ISAIAH 43:5 NIV

Think About It. . .

♡ Now is the time to accept what you can't change, keep a soft hand on his life, and pray unceasingly for your son. He's finding his own way. Leaving home was difficult for you both and returning home is often equally difficult. Rules come into play. . .your rules, and he's now used to fending for himself. Talk to him about it, and find some common ground.

♡ What bothers you most about your college-age son? What blesses you the most? Pray for what bothers you, and praise God for what blesses you.

♡ Keep the communication lines open, and avoid allowing your petty annoyances to frustrate you and shut him down (even if his room reeks of smelly workout clothes).

He returns home and chaos ensues. You love that he's home again and hate it at the same time. How can that be? That's normal. You have shifted from caretaker to spectator. He still has one foot in your door while he attempts to get his footing in the door of the world that awaits him. He needs to know house rules still rule when he returns home. Yet give him his space and support him with your love.

• •

9○. Gather the chipped plates, then let him go.

• •

"As soon as they learn to walk, they begin to walk away." Whoever made that statement knew what motherhood is all about—raising our sons to finally walk out of our lives.

For years Sara had prepared for that moment—the day her son would grow up and leave home in pursuit of a life of his own, apart from her. Having experienced this before with her firstborn, she thought she was ready. But she wasn't.

Her youngest child had graduated from college and taken a job in another state. So this time she not only faced a child's relocation, but a lurking empty nest.

She tried to make the transition as easy as possible. In an effort to help Matt get started on his new road of independence, Sara searched the house for items she thought he could use. Rummaging through the cupboards and basement became a journey back in time. An old couch, the kitchen set that she and her husband had since Matt was a baby, a few tray tables, and a smorgasbord of odd glasses and old dishes were set aside for him to take.

Out of all the items she gathered, however, none were as nostalgic as her hodgepodge of chipped plates and worn-out glasses from days gone by. Jelly jars converted into drinking glasses, outdated Ronald McDonald plates, and the Big-Gulp refillable glasses they never refilled, were among her finds packed and ready to go.

Then there were the plates and saucers with faded designs that they had used each day for more years than she could remember, representing precious moments in their lives. They were tangible reminders of the times her family prayed together, played together, cried and laughed together. Times that were about to end.

As Sara packed each disproportional stack of dishes in the box, a host of memories flooded her mind. Misty-eyed, she rested on a nearby chair, savoring the moment as if to recapture a glimpse of the past. She envisioned the little boy who sat at the kitchen counter, dunking cookies in milk as he finished coloring the picture that would grace her refrigerator door. Reflections of a simpler time held her captive as she smiled through the tears, recalling his childhood innocence.

Heavyhearted she returned to her work and continued to fill each box, realizing that an important chapter of their lives had ended and she had to let go. As she reached the top shelf of her kitchen cupboard, where she had replaced the old dishes with the new, she gazed at the brand-new, neatly stacked plates, uniform bowls, and matching glasses positioned in the same place the old ones just were. Resisting the change she thought, *But life isn't like that, Lord— all perfect and neatly stacked.* She longed for the days of mismatched glasses, scribbled artwork, sticky hands, and bruised knees.

Yet as Sara watched her son leave home, toting a box of careworn memories under her arm, she realized, *This isn't the end but a new beginning.* She somehow knew that her life would fill with new memories to cherish—moments when old jelly jars, chipped plates, and mismatched glasses would again line her kitchen cupboard, symbolizing yet another era, another new phase of life.

One season had ended, making room for another, and in her mother's heart she believed that more blessings were yet to come. It was time to let go and trust God. That meant loving her son enough to allow him to make his own choices, pave his own path, and chart his own course—trusting that the principles laid down for him throughout his childhood would stand. So that one day he, too, would build a cupboard full of memories, brimming with chipped plates and mismatched glasses. And you know what? That's exactly what happened.

This mom came to a startling but wise observation. Letting go of your adult son allows him, and you, to bloom. Your son leaving home isn't the end. It's a new beginning for you both.

Think About It. . .

- ♡ Is your "baby" leaving home? Are you struggling with a host of emotions? Remember, God gives moms seasons, and what you are experiencing is the end of one season and the birth of another.

- ♡ Help your son make moving easier. Apartment hunt with him, offer solicited suggestions, help him set up his kitchen, or just be available.

- ♡ A mother's memories are a treasure-trove. Cherish them, but move forward, knowing you have a whole lot more in store!

- ♡ It is much easier when your boy is a baby and you dedicate him to the Lord. At that moment, you give him to God but still cradle his tender life in your arms. But after years of holding him, instructing him, and loving him, the time comes to finally let your son go. Can you trust God now? Will you trust Him?

FINAL THOUGHTS:

Your son is venturing out on his own. And your mind reels with loads of questions, uncertainties, and worries. After all, the safety net of your loving care is removed. Now is the time to place him into God's hands with daily prayer. Keep in touch, make yourself available, but don't pressure him to visit often. If you do, he won't! Give him space and allow him to make his own way in the world.

91. Suffering from Empty-Nest Syndrome? Plan a date.

Do you devote a great deal of thought to what it'll be like when all of your children leave home? You're not alone. Statistics show that empty nest syndrome affects women primarily. And why not? As our little birds leave the nest one-by-one, our active parental role subsides if not ceases altogether. Our sense of loss and sadness often hurls us into a state of depression as we lose the identity we've held for eighteen long years.

When my first son left for college, I thought I had entered an emotional torture chamber. (See Tip 88.) After the twelve-hour drive to the college, we registered at the hotel across the street from the campus. The first night, our son had the option to stay in his dorm room—which resembled a walk-in closet furnished with a bed that I was sure came from the nearest penitentiary—or he could stay with us.

Our son's apprehensions tugged at my maternal heartstrings. His eyes told me he wanted to stay with us, but his I'm-at-college-now-so-I'd-better-do-the-adult-thing constrained him to make the closet his home.

Jimmy was always a homebody, so why did we think this would be an easy transition for him? As we said goodnight he walked away, pausing every few steps to look over his shoulder and wave. His face told me that he was already homesick, which made me feel worse than I already did.

After my husband, youngest son, and I returned to the hotel without Jimmy, I tried to think good thoughts. It didn't work. Instead, I flopped facedown on the bed and released my sadness in giant sobs.

The following day we said our final good-byes. I'll never forget the look on my son's face as we edged toward our vehicle to leave. Like an abandoned puppy, he stood alone in the parking lot, watching us until we disappeared from view. "I don't know if I can go through this again when Jeff leaves home for college," I confessed, choking back the tears. It felt as if someone had taken a sledgehammer to my chest, and everything in me begged to turn around, retrieve our son, and take him back home.

But four years later, saying goodbye to our six-feet-five baby went just fine. Unlike our first experience with Jim, Jeff was ready for college life, and we were ready for an empty nest. Though we shed a few tears, we shared a lot of smiles, too.

God prepares us for every experience we face with our sons. How we view each experience is what determines our attitude. Two people clanging around in a big house denotes loneliness to some. But by the time my second and last son left the nest, it was next to heaven for me.

Do you dread an empty nest? Are you grieving over the "loss" of your children? You haven't lost them, Mom. Believe me, they'll be back. Just in a different way than before. Change is difficult as we try to adjust, but it's also a blessing. This is the time of life that you and your husband have worked, sacrificed, and on many harried occasions, prayed for. You can finally date each other again!

Are you a new empty nester? Do you wonder how you'll ever adapt to a quiet, empty house? Rather than grieving for the past, look forward to the future. You'll adapt, and so will your son—quicker than you think! And in those moments of vulnerability when you mentally reminisce about the good old days, simply do what any good mother of grown kids would do. Plan your next date with your husband. Ah, empty nest.

A WORD FROM THE WORD:

"You will grieve, but your grief will turn to joy."
JOHN 16:20 NIV

Think About It. . .

♡ Some people, even your hubby, may not understand your sense of grief. But God does. Remember, you're not alone. Lots of moms have been through what you're experiencing now. It won't last, just like every other phase you've experienced as a mom. Give yourself time.

- ❤ Begin to plan ahead. Do something different, new, or out of the box.

- ❤ Talk to other new empty-nesters and plan get-togethers. Enjoy your freedom; avoid suppressing it with depressing thoughts.

FINAL THOUGHTS:

Although it may not feel or seem like it at this moment, eventually you will love your empty nest. Just as the above scripture notes, your grief will soon turn to joy! Wait for it. It's coming your way. God has a lot more in store for you in the days ahead.

92. Don't stop praying now!

The framed print, depicting a father kneeling at the bed of his sleeping son, was especially significant in our home. With head bowed, the dad placed his hand gently on his boy. In the background was an open window. The starry night reflected what takes place in the heavenlies when a parent prays for his or her child. An angelic being with uplifted arms guarded the home, pushing back the forces of evil that attempted to enter. The two entities engaged in what the Bible describes as spiritual warfare.

When our youngest son gifted us with the print, he told us it had reminded him of all the prayers we had prayed for him and his brother throughout their growing-up years. He was right on target! Prayer is powerful and the one and only spiritual weapon we have to combat problems and trials in our son's life.

The apostle Paul instructed the Ephesian church to clothe themselves in God's armor to fight against satanic forces. When we understand that the spirit world is more real than the temporal, and that without Christ we are helpless against demonic forces, we begin to exercise the privilege of prayer. Intercessory prayer summons the power of the Holy Spirit and God's angelic armies to fight spiritual battles on our behalf. Prayer calls upon God, and God answers.

Mom, where would you or your children be without prayer? From the time your son was small you prayed when he was sick, troubled, or dealing with problems. Heavyhearted, you prayed for your wayward teenage son. And long after he leaves home, you continue to pray for him, never relenting. To know that your son is a man of faith as a result of God's intervention is all a result of heartfelt prayer. You taught your son to pray from childhood on, and you continue to pray for him throughout his lifetime. Nothing replaces, or is as effective, as a mother's prayer for her child.

Is your son in need of prayer right now? Is he facing problems beyond his understanding or control? Has he departed from the Christian heritage in which you raised him? Is he immersed in the ways of the world or grappling with his faith? Do you feel as if you are helpless to do anything about it? Keep praying consistently.

If we could view the spiritual realm, we would realize the significance and power of steadfast prayer. The print of the praying father transports us into that reality. Despite how it may appear in the earthly realm, when you pray, God fights your battles. And He always wins. So put on that armor; you're equipped to fight.

A WORD FROM THE WORD:

Put on all of God's armor so that you will be able to stand firm against all strategies of the devil. For we are not fighting against flesh-and-blood enemies, but against evil rulers and authorities of the unseen world, against mighty powers in this dark world, and against evil spirits in the heavenly places. Therefore, put on every piece of God's armor so you will be able to resist the enemy in the time of evil. Then after the battle you will still be standing firm.
EPHESIANS 6:11–13 NLT

Think About It. . .

♡ As the familiar axiom goes, "Prayer changes things." It really does. Don't let discouragement rob you of your faith for your son's return to the godly principles you taught him.

♡ Pray daily for your son. You can't look into your son's heart and mind, but God can and does. He is working in ways you can't see. Prayer keeps the devil at bay and God's angelic forces in full military stance!

♡ Remind your son that you are praying for him and how much you love him. If your son resists God, don't take it personally. God doesn't. Rather, love him unconditionally and pray for him unceasingly. Then just watch God at work.

♡ If your son is facing difficulties in his life, be his prayer-support system. Let him know you'll stand in prayer for and with him.

FINAL THOUGHTS:

Don't wait for a problem to arise or for your son to fall on rocky ground before you uplift him in prayer. You've taught him to pray, and now he depends on your prayers, too. Oswald Chambers wrote: "We tend to use prayer as a last resort, but God wants it to be our first line of defense. We pray when there's nothing else we can do, but God wants us to pray before we do anything at all." Amen to that!

• •

93. Keep the toys your son treasures, even if they'll never score a bundle of cash.

• •

Going through your son's closet takes a wrecking ball and Job-like patience. Every son's mom knows that. After he leaves home, you sort through his things to give away or sell at your next garage sale, but you discover that letting go of his childhood things is almost as hard as letting go of him! Plus, when you ask your disinterested son, he does little to help you decide.

One mom kept most of her son's belongings far too long, even though every few years she'd survey her attic and basement to unearth boxes of stuff and then unload them somewhere else. Her lack of foresight to discern what to discard and what possessed the potential for future greatness and greenbacks amazed her.

She seemed to have a knack for ridding her kid's closet of toys that were worth money. Who would have known back in 1979 that grown adults would salivate over original Star War action figures in 2014? Or that certain tin lunch boxes would pack a whopping price today?

Nope. She dumped the valued toys and items and kept the noncollectible, no-interest toys like Lincoln Logs and a set of miniature soldiers complete with stockade and tiny spears. A faux pearl from her fake necklace served as a cannon ball to shoot from the miniature cannon. And, of course, she kept her two sons' first stuffed animals: "Boo-Boo," "Puppy," and an unnamed, hand-crocheted bear that had undoubtedly colonized untold numbers of dust mites.

As the mom pondered her foolhardy choices, her twenty-nine-year-old son stopped by for a visit. "Hey," he said with excitement, "those are my toy soldiers!" Sorting through the rubble, he leveled a look. "Mom, what happened to these guys?" he asked, examining the broken soldiers. Meticulously, he separated the intact soldiers from the broken ones.

"I'm not sure," his mom replied with a shrug and momentarily left the room. When she returned, she found her adult son sprawled across the floor. He had lined up the toy soldiers in a straight row and fired the pearl cannonball. "Hey, it still works!" he said in wild abandonment.

After properly teasing her son, the mom placed the toys back inside the box.

"I'll do it," he insisted, as he wrapped the soldiers in fresh tissue paper and re-boxed them in their safe, new living quarters. With an indelible marker he wrote, Tim's Soldiers in bold print on the exterior of the box.

Tim's mom instantly realized why she'd kept the world-worthless toy soldiers. These were valuable collectibles—swaddled in fond memories—to the one who had once spent hours in child's play with them, and nearly lost himself in adult child's play once again.

What's worthless to the world is priceless to your son—even as he ages. The same is true in his walk with the Lord. God's valuables, stored in the inner sanctum of the heart, possess the potential for abundant life and spiritual success. They are the only items worth seeking and keeping. Well. . .aside, perhaps, from a few toy soldiers.

A WORD FROM THE WORD:

Store your treasures in heaven, where moths and rust cannot destroy, and thieves do not break in and steal. Wherever your treasure is, there the desires of your heart will also be.
MATTHEW 6:20–21 NLT

Think About It. . .

💗 Before you discard your adult son's stuff, let him go through it and take what he wants. It will surprise you how many childhood memories those belongings will ignite.

💗 Your son and/or his wife may want to keep certain childhood items for their own son, things like your son's letter jacket or favorite toy. Ask them, or save items you think are pass-on-to-the-next-generation worthy. Think of the stories you could share about the items when your grandson gets older.

💗 Do you have something from your childhood you never discarded? Is it something you could pass on to your own children or grandchildren?

FINAL THOUGHTS:

In general, stuff is cumbersome. It takes up much-needed space and serves no good purpose. Have you ever determined to empty your closets or clean out the basement and afterward noticed you hardly made a dent in the stuff that had accumulated over time? The hardest part is knowing what to keep and what to ditch. Consider keeping a few of your son's treasures—perhaps the favorite toys that he's enjoyed—and getting rid of the rest. Or, better yet, make sure your kids take home one box of their "treasures" each time they visit. Eventually, your basement and attic will be a lot less crowded.

94. Ouch. Relax your hold.

Your son is out of the house and on his own. You've raised him the best you knew how, mistakes and all, and now it's time to sever the cord and allow him sink or swim. Ouch!

Corrie Ten Boom once told minister and author Chuck Swindoll, "You must learn to hold everything loosely. . . .even your dear family . . . . It will hurt you if He must pry your fingers loose." Are you experiencing the "ouch" factor? Is God trying to pry your hands open to release your son to Him? If so, remember that you must let go in order to let God do his work with, in, and through your son.

You've taught him to walk in God's ways, but is he? If he isn't, hold on to God, not your son. Bombard the gates of heaven with prayers for him daily. And don't give up! Love him unconditionally, refrain from preaching (it won't work anyway), and accept him the way he is, just as God accepts us all.

Perhaps as a child or teenager your son accepted Christ, and fell away. Regardless, God wants to reach him where he is right now, and He can't do it if you're in the way. Yes, you can actually get in the way. Don't abandon him; but don't rescue him either. God is his primary source now, not you. (Ouch again.)

One mom said that her son, Peter, was the ideal son growing up. Even during the so-called turbulent teens he stayed true to his faith in Christ and was a joy to raise. But after one year of college he dropped out, started drinking, and took drugs. Her heart crushed in disbelief and discouragement. *What happened to him? Where did I go wrong?* All these questions bombarded her like a military siege in the frontlines of war.

For seven years she prayed for Peter. Meanwhile, she had to stand back and painfully observe him sink deeper into sin, as he made one bad choice after another. When he came home for a visit, she loved him unconditionally and avoided questioning him about his lifestyle. That was a monumental feat for a concerned mom! But she understood that the more she interrogated him, the more he'd resent her, so any effort she made would produce zip. (Is the "ouch" factor intensifying?)

This mom's prayer, patience, and determination to "let go and let God" paid off. After years of irreconcilable mistakes, Peter recommitted his life to Christ. He returned to college while working full time and not only obtained his degree, but pursued a master's degree as well. He married and established a Christian home and later became the proud dad of a beautiful daughter. Today Peter is walking in God's truth, cognizant of his mother's prayers and, most of all, God's mercy.

Nothing means more to a Christian mom than to know her child is walking in the truth of the Gospel. But we can't make our offspring follow Christ. Our adult son must form his own personal convictions, and commit to abide by them. His relationship with Christ is personal, just as yours is. He might not embrace the same convictions as you do, nor do things the way you would. Accept that. He's an individual. Besides, the only One who has a monopoly on the truth is God.

Your son has to make his own way and bear the consequences of his own mistakes. He's learning, and so are you. So, let go and let God. He knows just how to reach and teach your son. What's more, He knows how to give you relief from the "ouch" factor.

A WORD FROM THE WORD:

I have no greater joy than to hear that
my children are walking in the truth.
3 JOHN 1:4 NIV

Think About It. . .

♡ What does it mean to "let go"? Don't nag or try to manipulate him into doing what you think he should do (even though you think you're right!). Realize he's no longer under your authority; he's under God's and accountable to Him.

♡ If you're asking, "What did I do wrong?" stop and consider this: God was the perfect Father, yet His children rebelled. It's not what you did wrong, it's what decisions your son has chosen to make.

💙 Continue with your life, doing what the Lord wants you to do. Pray for your son, support him when he reaches out to you, but stay within your boundaries.

💙 Speak less; pray more.

FINAL THOUGHTS:

All of his life you've been your son's advisor, teacher, disciplinarian, and go-to person. You are his mom. You've done it all and survived! When you let your son go, you release him fully and completely into God's capable hands. And you don't take him back. Keep praying for him; he relies on that. But allow him to follow his own course. Abraham Lincoln said: "All that I am or hope to be I owe to my angel mother. I remember my mother's prayers and they have always followed me. They have clung to me all my life." And so it is with you, your prayers, and your son's life.

• •

95. Expect your son to occasionally wear his foolish hat, even as an adult.

• •

Okay, this is not to say that boys are foolish. On the contrary. They are bright, witty, wise (some of the time), and adventurous. However, despite their age they seem to closet a foolish hat that every now and again appears on their head with little or no inducement. Even the most intelligent, sound-minded, well-rounded guys have one. Typically, they aren't even aware of this invisible piece of apparel—until a woman in their life points it out. And, Mom, you are the first woman in your son's life, so chances are you visualize the hat in living color.

The foolish hat entices boys to do mindless, unreasonable, nonsensical things. It's not their fault, really. It has to do with their inborn drive to test the limits, go the distance, and compete against others or themselves.

For instance: Your adult son vacations in Arizona and visits a desert nature preserve in the mountains. Despite park warnings about not leaving the well-traveled paths, your son does his own thing as the natural surroundings and his manly instincts morph into one. Suddenly, wham! He's off the beaten path in exploration of his own man versus nature adventure. Traveling solo, he ventures into the unknown, away from civilization and that breezy tram that transports reasonable-thinking folks from the top of the mountain to the bottom and back again. No, that's too touristy for your adventure seeker.

So there he goes. Your otherwise intelligent, successful, responsible son slips on his foolish hat and travels a desert path that leads to who-knows-where. Not only that, he carries one water bottle, and off-the-beaten-paths rarely have water stations available. His exploits heighten when he sees a rattlesnake for the first time. His stance is freeze framed to avoid a fatal bite. Now he's getting worried. Okay, so he has escaped that one but now notices his depleted water supply while the desert sun beats down at 100 degrees. He's hot, tired, and lost. Get the picture?

This type of behavior is not unusual for your big or little boy. It's normal. He dons his foolish hat and doesn't realize he has it on until he places himself in an awkward or, worse yet, dangerous position. His caveman instincts call him from the wild to the wild, the wilderness, or wherever adventure and exploration loom large.

From the time our sons are small we instruct them with safety measures. "Look both ways before crossing the street. Don't talk to strangers. Watch out for the other guy while driving." In an attempt to prepare them for every possible scenario, we offer—no, we indoctrinate—common sense suggestions liberally. (See Tip 72.)

Yet there comes a time when your advice no longer sticks (not that it did in the first place, but hey, we thought it might at the time). And since you can't accompany him everywhere, or hope that your repeated messages trigger cautionary measures in his brain, you must pray and leave him in God's hands. You hope that he'll remember your urgings. You pray for his safety. And you have faith that when he wears his foolish hat—and trust me, he will—that God will have mercy on him and help him out of the silly situations he inadvertently gets himself into.

Martin Luther King, Jr. noted: "Nothing in all the world is more dangerous than sincere ignorance and conscientious stupidity." Hats off to moms who warn their sons about the dangers of wearing stupid hats whenever inevitable bursts of stupidity and foolishness obliterate common sense.

A WORD FROM THE WORD:

And who knows whether that
person will be wise or foolish?
ECCLESIASTES 2:19 NIV

Think About It. . .

- ♡ Your son is old enough to know better, but he doesn't. Some things are learned from personal experience. All the teaching, nagging, and prodding in the world will often fall on deaf ears.

- ♡ Letting go of your adult son means allowing him to make his own choices. Wearing his stupid hat from time to time is one of those choices.

- ♡ The old saying, "You can lead a horse to water but you can't make him drink," holds true for your son, too.

FINAL THOUGHTS:

Humans are, well, human. Everyone makes foolish mistakes or decisions. Males often act before they think when it comes to challenges, competition, or risk taking. While you might see all the pitfalls and dangers, your son doesn't. He sees and revels in the thrill of the pursuit just like he did when he was a boy. Oy vey!

• •

96. Don't give up on your dreams for your son; God hasn't.

• •

Every mom harbors a dream for her son. As a Christian mom, you aspire for him to grow to spiritual maturity, emotional stability, and strength, and for him to develop and demonstrate Christlike characteristics. Yet sometimes our dreams—like a wall of rocks being battered by an ocean wave—take a beating and we wonder if our lifelong aspirations for him will ever come to pass.

Kevin was Jamie's firstborn, a joy to her heart. Throughout his childhood and, yes, even in his teenage years, he gave her little problems (shocking, huh?). But when he left for college he didn't just leave the nest. He fell from it face-first. He rebelled big time, and she was shocked, devastated, and confused.

She suffered indescribable heartbreak. From the day he was born, she had one desire for him: to mature spiritually and emotionally and to one day choose a spouse with whom he could share his life.

Kevin married outside the church and divorced one year later. Beaten down, he returned to the loving environment of his parents' home. Meanwhile, Jamie kept praying and loving her son. Finally one evening, Kevin and his then girlfriend knelt together. Before they prayed to accept Christ, Jamie had the honor of talking to them both about the Lord. Fast forward a year later: Kevin and his girlfriend married in a church ceremony that Jamie had always dreamed about for her son.

Throughout Kevin's turbulent years, his mom envisioned her son walking with Christ and one day marrying a Christian woman. For years Kevin made poor decisions. Despite his rebellion and recklessness, Jamie kept believing. Eventually through the trials he endured, the positive steps he took, and the spiritual commitment he made, Kevin allowed Jesus to transform him into a mature, God-fearing man. He and the love of his life stood before their pastor to exchange vows. They pledged to make Christ the head of their home, to pray with and for each other often, and to place God at the center of their union.

Only parents who have raised their son in a Christian home, helplessly watched him go astray, and then witnessed his return to his spiritual roots could understand what this church ceremony meant to Jamie and her husband. Their son's recommitment to God and Christ-centered marriage was an answer to a mother's prayer whispered late at night, many nights, at the foot of a tear-stained bed. It reaffirmed God's faithfulness and mercy. It symbolized the resurrection of a dream.

That doesn't mean that God answers every prayer with a yes or immediately. Although it is God's will to reach your son, He works with his free will. But He knows what it will take to draw him.

Before you pray, ask yourself, "Do my dreams align with God's will for my son?" Of course, some things are certain. We know it is God's will for your son to accept Christ and His forgiveness. But other issues aren't clear-cut in the scriptures. For instance, you might think your son should pursue a lofty career goal to gain financial security and prestige. But what is God's will for him? Has He called him to the mission field? Perhaps God wants your son to remain single, like the apostle Paul, available for God's work.

Don't give up on your dreams, especially if they are in line with God's will. God hasn't.

A WORD FROM THE WORD:

"For I will pour out water to quench your thirst and to irrigate your parched fields. And I will pour out my Spirit on your descendants, and my blessing on your children."
ISAIAH 44:3 NLT

Think About It. . .

♡ Have you given up on your dreams for your adult son? Does it seem as if your prayers go unanswered? Don't quit. Keep seeking God and, in the meantime, love your son back to Christ without criticizing him.

♡ God is the dream giver and the dream maker. Instead of aspiring for your son to live up to your dreams, aspire for him to live up to God's.

♡ When you back off—get out of the way—then God can work. If you constantly stand between your adult son and God, you unknowingly inhibit God's Spirit to reach him. Step aside, pray, and wait.

FINAL THOUGHTS:

Do you feel helpless? When your son was young you had a certain amount of control. After he became a young adult, your influence and involvement dissolved like a tablet of Alka-Seltzer in water. Keep praying for your son, and allow the Holy Spirit to do the work. Your work is pretty much done, but God's work has only just begun!

- -

97. Prepare yourself: He might return to the nest—repeatedly.

- -

"How are you enjoying your empty nest?" one well-meaning acquaintance asked Shannon.

"I have no idea," she stated flatly, "My sons keep returning home."

Just about the time you adjust to an empty house, begin to love your newfound freedom, and enjoy your husband again, your son moves back home. "I don't remember installing a revolving door," Shannon noted, "but it seems our adult sons have."

There was a time way back in the stone age of our childhood when leaving home went something like this: After you reached ages eighteen or nineteen, you left home only to return on college breaks or holidays from work until finally you moved out completely and happily (for sure by twenty-something) and jaunted down life's road to your own life.

That old-school mumbo jumbo dates the antiquated, unsophisticated, aging populations of yesteryear. Today's adult children leave, return, leave, return, leave, marry, multiply, and return again. This despite your attempts to teach them how to live securely and happily on their own. But perhaps there is a message hidden behind this revolving-door phenomenon.

Throughout our son's lifetime, we introduce personal independence through small mandates: "Brush your teeth." "Tie your shoes." "Do your homework." "Say your prayers." "Clean your room." All are limited measures of self-reliance given in manageable doses. We help him with menial tasks more often than not, hoping that one day he'll accomplish them on his own, without assistance and perhaps even without being told. (Is that possible?)

Then he matures and becomes independent. He has all the

answers. He knows his own mind and views life differently than we do and acts accordingly. We observe and bite our upper lip before blurting out criticisms or directives. Now his independent nature irritates us as we stand by—oozing with parental wisdom and experience—knowing he's headed for disaster. But we can't say anything—although if we're honest, we do most of the time anyway.

After reality chisels his false independence, we choke back an "I told you so" with a mixture of compassion and frustration. We listen and help him solve bigger problems than he ever had to master in algebra class. He thinks he's outgrown Mom, but he still returns when life and circumstances overwhelm him.

But think about it: Are we any different? Most of us do the same thing with God. We reach a stage of spiritual growth where we think we have the answers so we depend on Him less. Then reality slaps us into the realization that the only reliable source of comfort and help is our heavenly Father.

When your son leaves home, remember that he is constantly changing and maturing. The road to independence has potholes, and he might just hit a few. We all make mistakes, but those errors are stepping stones to maturity. Let him loose, and encourage his independence. If he moves back, set ground rules and make sure he is financially independent, apart from your pockets. But when and if he needs you—and he will—listen, encourage, pray, and offer loving support.

Shannon discovered that the revolving door stays with the home as long as loving parents reside there. Although she admits, "Nests are sure peaceful when the door loses its spin for a while!"

A WORD FROM THE WORD:

"There is hope for your future," says the Lord,
"Your children will come again to their own land."
JEREMIAH 31:17 NLT

Think About It. . .

♡ Has your son returned home under less than ideal circumstances? Love him unconditionally and hold him up in prayer. Avoid preaching to keep the lines of communication open. He'll confide in you when he's ready.

♡ Don't wait too long to set house rules for your son. After all, he chose to live under your roof. You can't control, nor should you, what he does on his own. But make it clear that while he's living with you he must abide by your rules.

♡ Help your son, but don't enable him. There's a difference. As the old adage goes, you can give people corn or teach them to raise their own crops. Which one is more beneficial to him?

FINAL THOUGHTS:

Various circumstances—finances, divorce, loss of job security, etc.—can cause your children to return home. Consider the prodigal son. He left home and squandered his inheritance. His friends left him, he was penniless, and he resorted to eating dinner with pigs. That's pretty desperate. The prodigal's father knew his son was destined for disaster when the young man left home, but that parent also knew the only way his son would learn was to release him to his own foolish devices. Consequently, the boy learned some hard lessons the hard way. Regardless, his loving father welcomed his prodigal home with open arms.

98. After your son leaves, avoid time gobblers.

Jason and Jan are empty nesters engaging in freedoms they seldom enjoyed when their boys lived at home. They eat meat loaf with onions, take spontaneous trips to Walmart for no reason at all, and leave town for overnight stays. They currently eat out, eat in, or don't eat at all if they so choose.

Jan confessed that the extent of their planning consists of matters such as: What weekend should we waterproof the deck? Is the wedding we have to attend this Saturday or next? Better pick up a gallon of milk; the one we bought two weeks ago is almost gone.

After twenty-six years of family responsibilities, the couple is enjoying a brief reprieve. Jan calls it "brief" because her past experiences have proven that circumstances change quickly. (See Tip 97.) Life is unpredictable, and who knows when the nip of adversity will bite at our heels.

You see, Jan and Jason are longtime members of the sandwich generation—namely, people caught between growing children and aging parents. So after twenty-six years of nurturing, teaching, worrying, helping, being there when no one else was, and praying when no one else did, the day finally arrived. It was time to expand and awaken subdued aspirations that Jan had filed in the "One day I will. . ." storage unit of her mind.

"I resent nagging obligations," Jan admitted, sipping a latte. "I've had a lifetime of them, so I bristle even when I have to wash the windows, listen to long-winded chatter, or attend borderline events that extract my time." Those who have raised their kids and cared for aging parents understand Jan. All her life she was the dutiful daughter and mother. Today she wants, and deserves, the opportunity to pursue or engage in something more venturesome than what's expected of her.

Maybe you feel the same as Jan. Time gobblers—people or things that distract you from what you'd really like to do in this stage of your life—pester and annoy you. Do you still experience the strangling noose of an untimely request or special favor? It's okay to covet your time and energy and become intolerant of activities void of personal meaning. After all, most of your life has blown in the breeze of the expectations of others, and of yourself. So you've earned the right to tread the road less traveled in pursuit of your pursuits!

That often means saying no gracefully without guilt; to follow lifelong dreams placed on hold; to lose oneself in a sea of soulful conversation, rather than on hollow chatter; to assist those who want help rather than help those who manipulate or control.

So how do you discard the time gobblers in your life? Here are a few empty-nester suggestions:

- ♡ **Say no politely, yet firmly.** Avoid the inclination to explain yourself.

- ♡ **Be open and honest with your feelings**. For instance: If someone asks you to host a Tupperware party and you feel that they are a salad-saver's waste of time, don't make excuses. Simply reply: "I'll have to pass on that one, but thanks for thinking of me." Direct, honest, yet polite.

- ♡ **Shed insecurities and unfounded guilt.** This is a tough one, but stand your ground without intimidation or unwarranted self-reproach.

- ♡ **Prioritize.** What do you value most? Time with your family? Time with God? Time to pursue career goals, a hobby, or just plain leisure time? The priorities of a twenty-five-year-old will differ greatly from an empty nester's.

- ♡ **Avoid excesses.** A good movie is relaxing, but too much television is a time gobbler.

- ♡ **Pray always**. Talk to the Lord about what's important to you and to Him. Seek Him for this phase of your life. Is there something He wants you to do?

Think About It. . .

- ♡ What activities or people gobble up your time and energy? Reassess your life and make necessary adjustments.

- ♡ Do you find yourself stuck in an emotional rut? You've raised your sons; it's time to break out of the doldrums and find new interests.

FINAL THOUGHTS:

Uncluttering your life of the things that smother you takes determination and backbone. The demands and expectations of others are your strongest rivals. You juggled kids, work, home, church, and all the extras with the expertise of a CEO (or a circus clown; often it's hard to tell which one). Flying in the face of unsolicited expectations is an act of bravery as you eliminate the time gobblers and begin living before life runs out! You've earned it. Take time for yourself and for your husband.

• •

99. He's finally grown; enjoy the fruits of your labor.

• •

I thought I had died and gone to parent heaven. Our future daughter-in-law invited my husband and me, along with her parents, to her apartment to discuss wedding plans. Beforehand, we ate dinner, following my son Jim's blessing. Afterward, Robin and Jim whisked back and forth to the kitchen, waiting on the four of us hand and foot.

My son cleared the table, balancing bowls, plates, and silverware in both hands. Not used to sitting idle at mealtime, I felt guilt emerge like an unexpected case of the hives. So I piled dirty plates atop one another and joined the twosome in the kitchen.

"Just set them down, Mom. We'll clean this up," Jimmy insisted as he loaded the dishwasher.

"Yeah, Mom," Robin echoed, "Go and sit down."

Go and sit down? We'll clean up? Is this the same son who used to plop down on the kitchen-counter stool, mutter, "What's for dinner?" and wait in a mummified state for me to fix his plate? What miraculous transformation occurred to change all of that? Maybe I could market it and make millions.

Happily, I returned to the dining room. Suddenly another transformation. Jimmy appeared with a bottle of Windex and paper towel to clean the glass table top. "Hey," he said, "why don't you guys sit in the living room and we'll serve dessert." I beamed with glee and pride. *This really is parent heaven,* I thought.

Years of serving meals, slaving over a hot stove, cleaning up his messes, chauffeuring him to and from athletic practices, praying for him, playing with him, and loving him eventually paid off. At times, I wondered if Jimmy would ever grow up. Servitude was never his strong point, and we had experienced some rocky years.

The Bible explains that we are the fruit of God's labor. Our children are the fruits of our labor, too—all those prayer-filled nights, instruction-laden days, and sacrificial ways. We dedicate ourselves to do what's best for our sons and pray for wisdom in raising them. To watch them ripen into maturity is one of the greatest joys of motherhood.

Today, Jimmy is a loving, caring, responsible Christian husband and father.

"Is there anything else I can get you, Mom," Jimmy asked from the kitchen. "More coffee? Or how about another piece of pie?"

"No thanks, Jimmy," I answered, "I'm full." *Actually my cup runneth over,* I thought.

A WORD FROM THE WORD:

You prepare a feast for me. . .You honor me by anointing my head with oil. My cup overflows with blessings.

PSALM 23:5 NLT

Think About It. . .

♡ Not all adult sons become adults. Thank the Lord if yours matured on schedule!

♡ What is "parent heaven" to you? A son who knows Christ? A son who reaches emotional and spiritual maturity? Or all of the aforementioned? God knows what blesses you the most, and He blesses you through your grown-up boy.

♡ All the giving, loving, and sacrifices are worth that one moment when you realize that your son has become who God intended.

FINAL THOUGHTS:

From the time you looked into your son's eyes for the first time, you wondered about his future. You prayed for God's wisdom to raise your little bundle of energy and joy. And you endured and survived! Finally, the day comes when your son becomes an adult. To know he knows Jesus comforts and blesses you. To realize he is a mature, godly man is everything you had prayed and hoped for. That's an overflow of blessings, for sure.

100. Embrace his wife.

Your relationship with your son has evolved and changed over the years. When he marries, it changes once again and forever. He has entered the most sacred union God has created between a man and woman. He and his wife are beginning a lifelong journey together to build a life and home.

Your role has changed. Sure, you'll always be his mom, but your relationship is different now. Not worse by any means, just different. View it this way: You've gained a daughter.

Is she the girl you would choose? In some cases, yes; in too many cases, no. But she's the young woman your son chose, so embrace her and welcome her into your family. The world jokes about the overpowering, domineering, busybody mother-in-law. Don't validate the world's idea of you. After all, do you really want to be known as the Marie Barone of the family?

It has been said that "no mother-in-law ever remembers that she was once a daughter-in-law." Remember what it was like when you married your husband? Did your mother-in-law show disapproval of you? How did that make you feel? Your daughter-in-law looks to you for acceptance. Don't disappoint, even if you don't agree with how she manages her household, the way she raises your grandchildren, or the manner in which she treats your son. That's his business, not yours. Pray for her, don't preach at her.

Support your son in his marriage. Don't bad-mouth his wife or pour out a list of complaints to him about her. If you have issues with his bride, talk to her with kindness and love. Build a positive relationship with your daughter-in-law. She, after all, is now the main woman in your son's life (whether or not you like the idea!).

As you embrace her, she will respond with respect and love. Chances are, you'll end up talking more to her than you will your son. That's actually normal. Phone your son to catch up on things, but not too much. Let him make the effort to contact you. If he hasn't talked to you in a while, try not to take it personally. And when he does call, avoid saying sarcastic, guilt-producing comments like: "Oh, so nice to hear your voice. I haven't talked with you in so long, I wondered if you still knew my number!" (Sounds like Marie Barone more and more, huh?) He's an adult now, Mom, and that's an immediate turn off to him. In fact, don't expect another call anytime soon after a few of those comments.

Remember that you are not in competition with his spouse. It's not about you; it's about them. You have supported and cheered for your son from the time he was small. Now you have two people to encourage and support: your son and his wife.

You have a lot to offer this young couple, but don't push, nag, or intrude. Love them, respect their boundaries, and pray for them. You have lots of wonderful family memories to cherish and so many more to create in this new phase of life for you and your son.

Think About It. . .

- You've raised your son to respect and protect women. In marriage, that's one of his primary responsibilities to his bride.

- Disagreements will occur. Handle them with care and love. As you cultivate a positive relationship with your daughter-in-law, good communication will result. If you express your feelings in an accusatory manner, you might ignite a bonfire. If you have issues to address, express how you feel without attacking her as a person. Avoid saying, "You did. . ." Rather say, "I feel. . ."

- Find a common bond with your new daughter-in-law. Does she enjoy shopping? (Who doesn't?) Does she like to cook? (Not everyone does.) Do you and she share a hobby? (If not, start one.)

FINAL THOUGHTS:

Remember that you'll always be your son's mom. He loves you. Yet he has a wife to love, cherish, and support now. Join him in that; don't fight him. The two have become one, just as you once joined with your husband in marriage. Be there for them both when they ask you. The best thing you can do for your son is to accept and love his wife.

101. Relax until your son becomes a daddy and makes you a grandma.

Where did the time go? Your son is grown; your job is complete. Now what? In the Book of Ephesians, the apostle Paul wisely instructed: "Having done all. . .stand" (6:13 NKJV). Or, in your case, sit. You deserve it. You've done it all from changing endless mounds of diapers to preparing him to leave home. From bruised knees to knee pads and beyond, you provided your son with love, nurturing, support, and discipline. You've worried about him, lectured him, fed him, and coddled him for eighteen years or (hard swallow) more.

Finally he's on his own, and you may or may not have an empty nest. If you do, it's time to refocus your attention. You've spent most of your adult life raising kids. Now it's your turn. Rekindle your relationship with your husband. It's probably changed a lot through the years. You'll have more time for one another, so enjoy it. Together, find things to do that you were unable to previously pursue because of the constant demands and responsibilities of motherhood. Join a couple's Bible study, take art classes together, reunite with old friends.

Refocus your energies. Is there something you always wanted to do but never had the time?

Do it now! Climb that mountain, take piano lessons, sew quilts, return to school, train for a marathon. The world is your oyster, as the saying goes. You have earned the right to focus primarily on *you* for a change. That in itself is an adjustment, but you'll get the knack really fast after you indulge in the freedoms that you can enjoy guilt-free.

This new phase of life may seem sad at first, so it's important to fill your days with new and different activities. Call a friend, attend a play, and have dinner afterward. While new moms often experience the "baby blues," seasoned moms undergo similar mood changes when their "baby" leaves home for good.

Enjoy the moment, because someday soon, your son may give you a grandson and the cycle will begin again—albeit in a totally different and wonderful dimension! The sounds of little boy feet pitter-pattering through your house will fill your heart and home with joy and excitement. Your windows and tabletops will once again be smeared with little fingerprints. You'll have stories to read to him and toys and biblical lessons to share.

Life comes full circle as motherhood evolves into grandmotherhood, seemingly overnight. So relax while you can, because grandbabies are your baby boy all over again—only this time, when he fusses or misbehaves, you can place him back into his daddy's arms. Ah yes, have a seat.

A WORD FROM THE WORD:

My people will live in safety, quietly at home.
They will be at rest.
ISAIAH 32:18 NLT

Think About It. . .

♡ Are you suffering from empty-nest syndrome? Consider some of the positive rewards of an empty nest: lower grocery bills, a cleaner house, no more staying awake until he comes safely home. Feel better?

♡ Have you wanted to start a home business? Embark on a new career. You have the time to invest in it now.

FINAL THOUGHTS:

The term *rest* doesn't necessarily mean the absence of activity; on the contrary, you might just engage in more activity than ever before. But it will involve what you want to do, void of looming responsibilities. So remove your hands from the wheel of your son's life and allow him to drive. Move into the passenger seat and enjoy the view for a change. You've done your part and then some. This is your time now. So sit back and rest in the nest!